VAN GOGH

His Life and Complete Works

FRANCESC MIRALLES

For this present English language edition:
Todtri Productions Limited, New York

Published by Longmeadow Press, 201 High Ridge Road, Stamford, CT 06904.

ISBN: 0-681-10473-2

Printed in Spain by
Fournier Artes Gráficas, S.A.

Editor:
Clotilde de Bellegarde

Designer:
Luis F. Balaguer

Editorial Assistants:
José Antonio Vázquez
Patricia Núñez Millieri
Rosa Vallribera i Fius
Albert Pujol Gámiz

English Translation:
Richard Jacques / Discobole

Design Assistants:
Manuel Domingo Pérez
Miguel Ortíz Català

Publishing Assistant:
Monserrat Juan Peña

Contents

Vincent Van Gogh lived just thirty-seven years, from 30 March 1853 until 29 July 1890, but they span what may have been the most enthralling human adventure in the history of 19th-century art. "I am a passionate man," he wrote once. But he was wrong: he was passion itself. He was a spirit tormented by lofty ideals to which he sacrificed his entire life. To approach Van Gogh is not to skim through the more or less interesting life of a painter, but to delve into the depths of a soul capable of giving up everything to communicate his deepest feelings. "I want to go so far that people will say of my work: he feels deeply, tenderly." And indeed he went that far; tortured for half his life in his attempts to pour out the full flow of his tenderness, but failing to find a way, and in permanent conflict for the other half. Painting works which barely found an echo among his contemporaries, he reached that unique state in which, as Antonin Artaud tells us, "When we see one of his pictures we forget that we are looking at a painting." For in fact what Van Gogh produced was not a coherent artistic output but a unique autobiography of his feelings.

Vincent left us that autobiography in two different media – literature and painting – so closely interlinked that the one cannot be understood without the other. For eighteen years he wrote ceaselessly to his brother Theo and to his sister Wilhelmina and his painter friends Van Rappard, Émile Bernard, and Paul Gauguin. For ten years he painted at a frenzied pace. Over a thousand letters, more than one thousand two hundred drawings, and nine hundred oil paintings were his legacy.

With Vincent everything is closely interrelated – his correspondence and his painting, his life and his feelings – so much so that he inspired Karl Jaspers to write: "In this exceptional being, the personality, the activity, the morality, the life, and the work compose an indissoluble whole, so homogeneous that it is not easy to find comparable cases."

To understand the life of this genius we have to bear two things in mind: his relationship with his brother Theo and his illness. Vincent's life – essentially aggravated by his precarious economic situation – could only follow its path because of the material and moral care given to him by his brother, four years younger than he, who gave him money to survive, advised him constantly, and made sacrifices to help him. To the point that in the last letter Vincent wrote him, found in his pocket after his death, he went so far as to say: "Through my mediation you have your part in the very production of certain canvases which

Van Gogh's copious correspondence (over 800 letters) shows that for him writing was a need and part of his artistic work. Vincent's letters to his brother Theo and his friends (in this case, Anthon Van Rappard) are a mixture of his life and his everyday work.

keep their calm even in disaster." Theo was Vincent's haven in time of trouble.

Then there was his illness. That famous madness which fades away in the face of the powerful personality of a man without equal. Paul Signac wrote, "He never gave me the impression that he was demented. Although he hardly ate, he drank excessively. When he returned from a day under the blazing sun, in the torrid heat, as he did not have a proper home in the town he used to sit on the terrace of a café. Absinthe and brandy followed one another in quick succession. How could anyone stand up to that? He scarcely ate. He was charm personified. He loved life passionately. He was an ardent and a good man."

But those testimonies are clouded by the theories of syphilitic dementia propounded by some, or the schizophrenia diagnosed by others. Nonetheless, there has recently been an increasingly strong belief that Vincent had a hereditary epileptic psychosis aggravated by personal circumstances such as possible syphilis, alcoholism, malnutrition, or exhaustion. And so Vincent was not mad.

The positive presence of his brother and the negative presence of an afflicting disease were decisive in conditioning the life of this irascible, solitary, tender, fascinating genius. For that reason his biography has to be a mixture of personal details and states of mind, of his artistic successes and his inner struggles, since only by approaching Van Gogh in his entirety, as a person, can we understand his art and the process of his accomplishments.

Vincent Van Gogh, the son of Theodorus Van Gogh and Anna Cornelius Carbentus, was born on 30 March 1853 in Groot Zundert, a small village in the Brabant region of Holland. He was the eldest of six children, although a year before he was born his mother had given birth

The house where Vincent Van Gogh was born in the Dutch town of Groot Zundert. The painter is said to have been born in the room on the first floor on the right. At the age of 11 he was sent by his father as a boarder to Zevenbergen, where he studied French, English, and German. From there he went to the Hannik Institute in Tilburg until 1868 when, owing to financial problems in the family, he had to return to Groot Zundert and abandon his studies.

to a child whom they named Vincent, who lived only a few days. Van Gogh acquired a rather irregular early education, though it was no different from that of many children at the time. He went for a year to the parish school in the village, spent two years at a boarding school in Zevenbergen, and a year and a half at a secondary school in Tilburg. He was an averagely well-behaved and studious pupil, and acquired the habit of reading, which he kept up throughout his life and which made him a very cultured person. For many years he liked to read novels about the poor, the peasants, and the persecuted to corroborate the poverty and suffering he saw in the people around him. He was taciturn and used to escape on his own for long country walks to look at nature. He would pick up animals to examine and study, and he collected wild creatures, plants, and birds' nests. His brothers and friends regarded him as the wisest of them all and respected him accordingly. After those years of elementary schooling, he spent a year and a half at home studying nature and reading until his sixteenth birthday. Then the family decided that he had to work and found him a place at the branch of Goupil in The Hague. His uncle was a partner in the firm, which he had owned until he sold it to the famous French art dealers. Young Vincent did his duty at work though he was not a lover of trade, but he had his reward in the shape of several promotions. He was first transferred to Brussels, next to London, and finally to Paris. In Brussels he received a visit from his brother Theo, who was fifteen. That was the beginning of the deep friendship that was to bind them all their lives; their correspondence began as soon as Theo left. In London he fell in love with Eugénie Loyer, his landlady's daughter, who turned down his proposal of marriage. It was his first disappointment in love and it left him in a state of prostration. He was moved to Paris, and to compensate for his frustration, he began to read the Bible avidly. On 1 April 1876 he was dismissed for irregular conduct and lack of interest in his job.

If his years at school left him with a deep love of reading, his time in business inspired him with an impetuous passion for art. And his religious fervor grew. After working in a school in Etten and a

Photograph of Vincent Van Gogh when he was 18. From the age of 16 to 23, the artist worked in The Hague, Brussels, and London for Goupil, an art dealer. His passion for painting dates back to that period when he frequented the museums in those cities.

Engraving of miners which appeared in L'Illustration. *Living in the Borinage and sharing the miners' life, Vincent described them in these words: "A curious sight these days to see, in the evening, around dusk, the miners passing by against a background of snow. They are all black when they come up out of the pits in the light of day; they look like chimney-sweeps."*

bookshop in Dordrecht, he moved to Amsterdam to study to become a priest. However, he refused to study Latin and Greek because they were no longer spoken and decided to work as a lay preacher in the Borinage. He settled in Pâturages and lived with the miners of that grim region in a spirit of total self-sacrifice. He was sent to Wasmes, where he lived in a hut and slept on straw, giving away all he had to the poor. His zeal annoyed his superiors, who reprimanded him. He was transferred to Cuesmes, where he continued to deprive himself of everything and live on bread and water to be closer to the poor. But his example was once again troublesome; he was accused of excess and his licence to preach was withdrawn. His behavior was openly antisocial. The two long years in which he developed his true evangelical spirit in its full purity were not understood. One of his sisters told him, "Piety has made you an idiot." No-one realized that he was not trying to cultivate antisocial behavior; he was living what he saw before him with great passion, which can be dangerous if carried to extremes.

He then decided to dedicate himself to art, which he could work on in solitude. With hardly any money he left for Courrières to visit Jules Breton, a painter he admired. After walking for a week he reached his new studio, built of red brick, "with a Methodist regularity and a cold, inhospitable, irritating aspect." He left without even knocking on the door. "From that moment everything seemed different to me." It was the first time that he had chosen his destiny. It was August 1880.

In July that year Vincent wrote Theo a long letter after several months' silence; it marked the definitive reconciliation of the brothers. The letter sets out his future path with unusual clarity: first he decided to break

with his family once and for all – though two years later he returned to live with his parents – as he had become "an impossible, suspicious kind of person, someone that is not worthy of trust." He speaks of the mysticism he was to nurture all his life: "What happens within seems to be happening without. Someone may have a burning fire in his soul and no one comes to warm himself by it; those who pass by see only a plume of smoke rising from the chimney and go on their way." He then tries to justify from deep inside himself his dedication to painting, which is also apostolic: "You see, it's just that there are many things which have to be believed and loved; there is something of Rembrandt in Shakespeare and of Correggio in Michelet and of Delacroix in Victor Hugo and then there is something of Rembrandt in the Gospels and something of the Gospels in Rembrandt; however you see it, everything becomes more or less the same provided you have a good understanding of things... Try to understand the last word of what the great artists, the most serious masters, say in their works of art and you will see God in them. Someone has written or said it in a book and another in a painting." And he would always be a rebel: "But respectable people are stranger than you might think at first sight. Now, one of the reasons I am out of place – I have been displaced for years – is simply because I have different ideas from those gentlemen who give jobs to people who think as they do. It is not just a pose, as people have reproached me hypocritically; it is a more serious question, I assure you." As Vincent said, he had changed his feathers, like the birds; he knew he was a loner, that he would be a rebel and that his work would have the value of an apostolate. Counting, of course, on the unconditional support of his brother Theo,

Since his time in Belgium and his meeting with Anton Mauve, Vincent had been collecting engravings which he cut out of magazines. He admired and copied the paintings of Millet, such as The Gleaners *(Louvre Museum, Paris), reproduced here, which influenced him in the process of incorporating the theme of the peasants.*

he began to follow the only piece of advice Theo had given him – to learn artistic technique thoroughly. He went to Brussels in October 1880 to attend the free Academy of Fine Arts. We know nothing about his time there, except that he drew with great intensity from treatises on anatomy and copied the prints that Theo sent him, mainly by Millet. He met Anthon Ridder Van Rappard, a young painter with whom he had a close friendship for five years – we have a large number of letters from Vincent to him – which was broken off by his criticism of *The Potato Eaters*.

However, when Vincent died, Van Rappard wrote, "Anyone who had seen that life of effort, struggle, and pain could have felt only sympathy for a man who demanded so much of himself and ruined his body and mind. He belonged to the caste from which great geniuses emerge."

On 12 April 1881 he returned to Etten to his parents' house and drew the country people, the women working in their houses, and nature. There he sought a form of expression which leads to the essence of things, from their outer shape to their inner meaning.

In early summer his cousin Kee Vos came to spend a few days at their house. She was a widow with a four-year-old daughter. Vincent fell in love with her. A fresh disappointment; he was rejected again. Kee returned to Amsterdam and Vincent travelled to see her, but in vain. He went to The Hague where, he showed his drawings to the dealer Teersteg, reputed to be one of the leading experts in Holland. Total silence. He showed them to Anton Mauve, a fashionable painter married to a cousin of his, who encouraged him and persuaded him to paint some still lifes in oil. They were his first paintings and they have fortunately survived. But their relationship was severed the day he smashed the plasters

In 1883, Vincent settled in Nuenen with his parents, who provided him with the studio in the garden of the family rectory in the photograph. Here Van Gogh worked away until the death of his father. Afterwards, he moved his studio to the sacristy of the village church, which he painted so many times.

Mauve had suggested as subjects, arguing that he wanted to paint life. In The Hague he started to forget his cousin Kee, but "I cannot, it is impossible for me to live without love. I am a man with passions. I have to find a woman or I shall freeze and turn to stone." And he found Clarine Maria Hoormik, whom he called Sien; she had posed for him as a model, she was thirty-two and had worked half her life as a prostitute. Vincent took her and her little girl into his studio. Their union vitalized the artist's spirit but weakened his body, as three people could not live on the money he had and keep up his painter's studio as well. After various helping hands from his brother and after Sien had another child, she left him when he suggested going to live in the country. In The Hague the artist's love life ended. He left us some delicate drawings of Sien and the well-known *Sorrow*, one of his few lithographs.

On 11 September 1883 he left for Drenthe, where he stayed for less than three months. He travelled the area and enjoyed nature but began to feel lonely and anxious and returned to his parents' house; they were living in Nuenen at the time. It was just two years since his father had thrown him out.

He stayed there for two years. It was a decisive stage of his training. Until then he had painted about thirty oils, but by the time he left he had done two hundred. It was the time of profound study of color which he observed in the Dutch classics.

His relations with his family were up and down. In spite of his parents' scepticism about his painting, they set up a space for him in a building in the garden to use as a studio, though he rented two rooms in a nearby house to be more independent. When his mother broke her leg shortly after he arrived, he looked after her and did drawings – he called them trifles – to amuse her.

But the artist's independent life clashed constantly with the social habits of the family and the small village. He was an oddity who could be blamed for everything. So when Margot Begemann, a forty-year-old spinster neighbor, fell madly in love with Vincent and poisoned herself when the feeling was not requited, everyone blamed the painter, though nobody was in favor of the relationship. When an organist friend agreed to give him piano lessons and the painter began to compare notes with colors – a comparison that obsessed him throughout his life – the old master abandoned him because he thought the idea was mad. When a young woman who had been a model for him – it seems that she was the girl with her back turned in *The Potato Eaters* – became pregnant,

During the winter of 1884-1885 in Nuenen, Vincent tirelessly painted heads of peasants and wrote to Theo: "I have been busy painting those heads. I paint by day and draw by night. That way I have painted at least thirty and drawn as many." The work is reflected in his letters, which are full of profiles.

everyone accused the painter, who had nothing to do with it, and the Catholic priest forbade his parishioners to pose for him. The atmosphere in Nuenen, like everywhere he ever lived, became unbreathable for him.

If in The Hague his uncle Cor had commissioned him to do twelve drawings of the city, in Nuencn a locksmith asked him to decorate his dining room. He made no money out of the commission, but it allowed him to work without spending any money. And it gave him confidence.

In Nuenen he gave painting classes to some young people and a few friends who wanted to occupy their leisure time. He took them to the fields and exhorted them to paint without retouching; "do not try to beautify it," he told them. He began to be obsessed with the haste, the speed of execution which would be one of his priorities and with which Gauguin would reproach him.

On 26 March 1885 Vincent's father died suddenly at the door of the house. The death inspired several works with clear allusions to his progenitor. The most incisive is the one which shows a large Bible open next to a novel by Zola – the confrontation of father and son, of tradition and modernity, of law and life. Spurred on by his father's death, Vincent produced one of his masterpieces, the most complex composition of figures he ever did and the most academic. "It could be said that this is a real painting of peasants. I know it is," he wrote proudly, as his spiritual obsession was still the peasants and the workers, and his thematic obsession was to depict them more accurately, if possible, than Millet, whom he so admired.

The Potato Eaters lies between two personal frontiers – between the apprentice and the professional and between the dominance of dark color and the dominance of light color. Though the artist himself was not aware of all that, he considered it his most important work and allowed no criticism of it. Indeed, the harsh words of Van Rappard brought about the end of their friendship.

Nuenen was the decisive stage for Van Gogh. He had more peace and quiet but he lacked contact with other artists. And as the atmosphere was unfavorable, he decided to leave. His mother and sister also left the village shortly afterwards and their lack of interest in Vincent's work was such that hundreds of drawings and paintings he had done there were lost.

Once he had settled in Nuenen, he painted, among others, a picture of Peasants Digging Potatoes, *of which he sent this sketch to his friend Van Rappard in a letter.*

Antwerp was a stopover of three months – from 24 November 1885 to 27 February 1886. It was a brief but highly positive parenthesis for both his artistic career and his life. He discovered Japanese prints, which he began to collect and which influenced his use of line and color. Antwerp brought fresh encounters with Rembrandt for feeling and Franz Hals for color. And the revelation of Rubens, who "tries to really represent and express, even though his figures are sometimes hollow, an atmosphere of joy, serenity, grief, through a combination of colors." He learned some important lessons.

He knew he had left his family and Holland forever, and that he was alone with Theo. He knew that his way of being and doing was systematically rejected – his rejection by the teachers and students at the Academy of Fine Arts was total – and he knew that he would go hungry and suffer all kinds of difficulties: "I look as if I have spent ten years in prison." Vincent knew all that and wrote: "I am on the road to find what I am looking for." And he left for Paris, leaving Theo no choice but to receive him. He arrived in Paris on 28 February 1886 and spent just two years there. The first months were peaceful. Theo even wrote to his mother: "If we could go on living together like this... I think the most difficult time is past and that he will find his way."

In Montmartre, Vincent discovered Impressionist painting, shared the bohemian life of the artists of the day, like Toulouse-Lautrec, and was a regular at the gatherings in cafés, such as the one in the photograph, in the garden of which he painted Pleasure Garden in Montmartre.

Accompanied by other painters, such as Paul Signac, Vincent often went to paint the outskirts of Paris. They used to take the tram to Asnières, where several Impressionists met to paint colors. It was there, in 1887, that he did this Restaurant de la Sirène *(Musée d'Orsay, Paris).*

He hastened to enter the studio of Fernand Cormon, a painter of historical subjects and an academician, but recognized as a good teacher. Here too his way of painting, his brush dripping, applying the paste with his fingers, splashing everywhere, left his fellow-students astounded. In Paris he met Toulouse-Lautrec and shared his friendship and adventures; and Émile Bernard, with whom he shared a studio in Asnières and to whom he always continued to write.

Paris was a place for friends and acquaintances: Pissarro, Gauguin, and Signac, who all marked his life and work in quite different ways; Anquetin, Seurat, Cézanne, and Suzanne Valadon. Their work made a powerful impact on him. The Impressionism and Pointillism he had seen in the magazines he was now seeing at firsthand, and the painters who practiced the techniques were his friends. Millet, whom he never ceased to admire, seemed too dark compared with Monticelli and Delacroix and with his own friends. He gradually became closer to them, but without losing his own personality, which he maintained even in his themes.

Paris was the height of his passion for Japanese style; he drew as many lessons from the prints as from the work of his colleagues. It influenced his handling; he included reproductions of Japanese prints in his canvases and had a show at the restaurant Le Tambourin, where some of his works were hung as a permanent collection.

Paris was a harmonious relationship with "Old Tanguy", who sold painting materials and exchanged his products for the unsalable canvases of the young painters. Apart from painting his portrait, Van Gogh became an intimate friend of his; they felt the same about many things. And Paris was the relation with Agostina Segatori, the owner of Le Tambourin, where Vincent brought together all the young painters of the moment, like an artists' club, in spite of the dubious reputation of the establishment.

But time was never on Van Gogh's side. He occupied the whole of the apartment he shared with his brother, even though they had moved to a slightly bigger one; he attacked Theo constantly because as an art dealer he was clearly a representative of the bourgeois oppressors; and he could not bear to be contradicted on any subject. "My life at home is practically unbearable; nobody wants to come and see me any more," Theo confessed to his sister Wil. Vincent's nervous condition was a sign that Paris no longer had anything to offer him. He could not write any more: "...the French air clears the brain and does you good, a great deal of good," as it

Self-Portrait. *Paul Gauguin (Musée d'Orsay). In his memoirs, Gauguin speaks of Vincent's insistence that he should move to Arles: "At the time I was working in Pont Aven in Britanny and whether because the studies I had begun tied me to the place or because a vague instinct warned me of something out of the ordinary, I resisted for a long time until the day when, conquered by Vincent's sincere gestures of friendship, I set out."*

had when he arrived in the city. The air of Paris no longer did him good because he was not a man of the city and he had already come to the end of all Montmartre had to offer him. He painted flowers repeatedly – he embarked on the theme of the sunflowers – to abandon the gray ranges and get used to a scale of bright colors. He had painted from a heterodox position using Impressionist, Pointillist, and Symbolist concepts without adopting their themes. He left with a much lighter palette. But he needed the country and more light. As usual, he left when he felt his environment was drained.

A Wagner concert, which the brothers went to the night before Vincent left for the South, marked the end of that period which had brought so much to that genius, still generally despised. Van Gogh's strength was in his passion; his charm in his dreams. "I came to the South for a thousand reasons. I needed to see a different light, I thought that by looking at nature under a brighter sky I could reach a truer idea of the way the Japanese feel and draw." Vincent arrived in the city of Arles in Provence on 20 February 1888. Arles was the Japanese dream because of its colors. Arles was the dream of setting up the community of artists which had occurred to him in Drenthe and whose structure he had begun to manufacture in Paris. Arles was to be his maturity and the beginning of the end, owing to that intransigent lack of understanding which his uninhibited behavior always aroused.

In Paris he had discovered color; in Arles he discovered light. That light which sings in a thousand notes in his paintings and his letters: those bronze golds, old golds, those blues and yellows – the yellows! – and purples which transform them. That transparency of the air which picks out color in the distance. Vincent exulted inwardly and, as usual in such cases, his health improved as far as it could, since he ate little and wretchedly.

It was the sunflowers which bound together his feelings at that moment. Dazzling yellow, like a synthesis of the new light. "A light which, for want of a better word, I can only call yellow." It was the trees in blossom, like the ones he gave his sister-in-law Jo when her child was born: "...the trees are in blossom and I would like to do a monstrously happy Provençal orchard."

Of the intense Provençal nights, which thrilled him with their stars, he left unequalled records in *The Night Café*, *The Starry Night on the Rhône* and others. "I often think that the night is more alive and richer in color than the day." And to sum up his new state of mind: "Now I just enjoy."

The Yellow House is not just an extraordinary painting; it is an image of his home in the South. He rented it, painted it, decorated it, and furnished it with unexpected care for a person so little given to refinement. The fact is that the yellow house meant the realization of that dream of founding a community of artists where, living with monastic asceticism, they would discuss art, organize a new system of selling their works and share communally everything material and spiritual.

He thought Gauguin's arrival would signal the beginning of the fulfillment of that wish. But Gauguin was a practical man who came to Arles basically to keep Theo happy so that he would continue to sell his works, as by then he was also in tight straits. But Gauguin, in his haughtiness and self-confidence, could not understand the sensitivity of such a defenseless, passionate and tender spirit as Vincent. With a stupefying lack of understanding, Gauguin wrote: "I undertook the task of straightening things out for him, which I thought would be easy as I was in a rich and fertile land... since that day my Van Gogh made astonishing progress." Naturally, anyone capable of writing like that must have provoked the impulsive, violent Van Gogh. Vincent made him nervous. The episode when Vincent threatened Gauguin in a final, fateful quarrel was a spectacular, notorious incident, a result of the enormous tension which Paul Gauguin's lack of sensitivity and esteem created in Vincent Van Gogh. The yellow house of the "artists' community" had no future because the man who could have set it in motion had sunk it beyond recovery.

Vincent had an important collection of Japanese woodblock prints. From the Hiroshige series, to which this Rice Field *belongs, Van Gogh copied this* Bridge in the Rain.

Je vous demeure bien obligé de votre
amicale et bienfaisante visite qui
m'a considerablement contribué à me
remonter le moral
Je vais bien maintenant et je travaille
à l'hospice ou dans les environs.
Ainsi je viens de rapporter deux
études de vergers.

En voici croquis hatif — le plus grand
est une pauvre campagne verte à petites maisons
ligne bleus des alpines ciel blanc à bleu
le devant des clos aux haies de roseaux où de petits
pechers sont en fleur — tout y est petit les jardins
les champs les jardins les arbres même ces montagnes
comme dans certains paysages japonais c'est pourquoi
ce motif m'attirait
L'autre paysage est presque tout vert avec un peu
de lilas et de gris — par un jour pluvieux
Bien aise de ce que vous dites que vous vous êtes
fixé et serai désireux d'avoir encore de vos nouvelles
comment le travail marche/, comment est le caractère de ces
parages là.

At each stage of his life, Van Gogh had someone near him who could understand his inner being. In Arles it was the Roulin family. Joseph Roulin was the station postman. His anarchic spirit chimed perfectly with Vincent's and until he left for his next destination in Marseilles at the end of January 1889 he never left his friend's side, nor did his family. Vincent painted portraits of all of them.

Towards the middle of December 1888 the tension between Van Gogh and Gauguin reached its limits and was further aggravated by the turn of events. When Vincent realized that his friend was about to abandon him, tragedy struck; he tried to attack him with a razor, but cut off one of his own ears, which he delivered to a prostitute friend. At first Gauguin was accused of murdering him when he was found unconscious. The whole incident caused an upheaval in the little town, which had absolutely no sympathy for the foreign painter. Later on, a group of citizens demanded that he be shut up in a mental sanatorium.

In the spring of 1889 on one of his outings from the hospital in Arles, Vincent worked in the country and did the two studies of orchards the sketches for which are reproduced here. He sent them to Paul Signac, saying: "Everything here is small,... The gardens, the fields, the trees, even the mountains, as in some Japanese landscapes..."

From his arrival in Arles, Vincent painted the Langlois bridge, a motif which he repeated on numerous occasions. Indeed, since he began to paint, the repetition of themes – peasants, weavers, faces, flower vases, sunflowers – had been a constant in his work.

24 December 1888 was the beginning of a long cycle of crises, collapses, recoveries, bouts of depression and exhaustion, work and passionate enthusiasm which lasted until the end of July 1890. First, he was admitted several times to Arles Hospital, where he was visited by Roulin and Paul Signac. They also went to see the yellow house. But on 8 May 1889 he had himself temporarily shut up in the Saint-Paul-de-Mausole asylum in Saint-Rémy-de-Provence, where he stayed for a year, until 16 May 1890. The continuous ups and downs of that year, in the heart of nature in Provence, may be typified by these two statements: "Both in life and in art I can do very well without God; but without suffering I cannot do without something far greater than I am, something which is my whole life: the strength to create." Painting was what allowed him to survive. "You will find that this may be the painting I have done most patiently and best; it is painted with calm and great assuredness of brush strokes. The next day I collapsed like an animal," he said of the picture he gave his sister-in-law for the birth of his nephew. But painting struck him down again and his state of health fluctuated constantly.

However contradictory it may seem, living with the mentally sick – not many of them, as the number of inmates at the time was never more than fifteen – made him lose his fear of madness, an illness which everyone, including himself, believed he had. He describes the center, which was somewhat precarious in terms of facilities and food, but he speaks with great affection and tenderness of the inmates who, he says, show more politeness and tact than the inhabitants of Arles. "Before those beings repelled me and it was devastating for me to think that so many people of our profession, Troyon, Marchal, Méryon Jundt, Maris,

Monticelli and a whole lot more, had ended up like that. I could not even imagine them in that state. Well! Now I think of all that without fear; that is, I do not find it any more atrocious than if they had died of something else, of consumption or syphilis, for example. I see those artists recover their serene bearing."

He could paint and had a room of his own. He also painted in the garden, of which he captured many different aspects – on occasion he said that he represented it as it must have been before in its splendor – and painted outside when he was allowed to go out with an escort.

Vincent was interned at a special moment of his professional career. At the end of January 1890 Theo sent him a long article by the critic Albert Aurier published in the first number of *Le Mercure de France*, in which he analyzed his work in detail: "It is the universal, mad, blinding blaze of things; it is matter, the whole of nature twisted frenetically, in a paroxysm, raised to the highest point of exacerbation; it is form which turns to nightmare, color which turns to flames, lava and precious stones, light which turns to fire; life, high fever..." He was pleased with the article, although he admitted that the merit was not his, as he owed so much to Monticelli, Gauguin, and his friends in Paris. Another encouraging piece of news: at the Salon des XX in Brussels, his canvas *The Red Vines* had been sold for 400 francs, a sale which was neither the first nor the last, contrary to popular belief.

Everything indicates that he was on the verge of success. But Vincent did not pay much attention. He kept painting, bringing us the most thrilling visions of the cypresses of Provence ever to beput on canvas.

Old photograph of the Café d'Arles, the yellow house, on the top floor of which Van Gogh went to live when he arrived in the town. In May 1888, Vincent wrote to Theo: "Today I rented the right wing of the building, which has four rooms, or rather two with two closets... I hope I have been lucky this time, you know – yellow outside, white inside, in full sunlight, I shall finally see my canvases in a well-lit interior."

When he was confined to the Saint-Paul-de-Mausole asylum in Saint-Rémy-de-Provence, Vincent drew the garden, the only open-air theme he had access to without supervision.

But he began to think about returning to the North, as if he had a presentiment of his death. It was his friend Pissarro who suggested he should move to Auvers-sur-Oise near Paris, the home of Doctor Paul Gachet, an art lover, who would take care of him. On 17 May 1890 he arrived in Paris, where he spent three days in Theo's house, met his nephew and was visited by Pissarro, Toulouse-Lautrec, and Tanguy, among others.

On 21 May he reached Auvers and moved into the Auberge Ravoux – today the Auberge Van Gogh – and as usual when he made a change he was in good spirits and worked intensely. He made friends with Doctor Gachet, whose portrait he painted; he also painted the surroundings, including one masterpiece: *The Church at Auvers*.

But in late June a letter from Theo came to shatter his peace of mind and his projects. Theo had problems with work, and he and his wife were growing weaker physically. Vincent feared being abandoned. He visited his brother in Paris, but the visit did nothing to calm him. He returned to Auvers and broke off relations with his doctor. "...I try to be happy, but my life is also threatened at its very roots and my steps falter too."

He painted the impressive July cornfields. "They are vast stretches of wheat beneath stormy skies and I have had no difficulty expressing their sadness and extreme loneliness." Sadness and loneliness. A new depression, and on 27 July, in the countryside, he shot himself in the stomach. He managed to walk back to the inn. Theo arrived from Paris.

Inner courtyard of the Saint-Paul-de-Mausole sanatorium, where Vincent had two adjoining rooms at the request of his brother Theo; he used one of them as a painting studio. Van Gogh's only concern during his stay at the sanatorium was to paint; for him, the illness did not count.

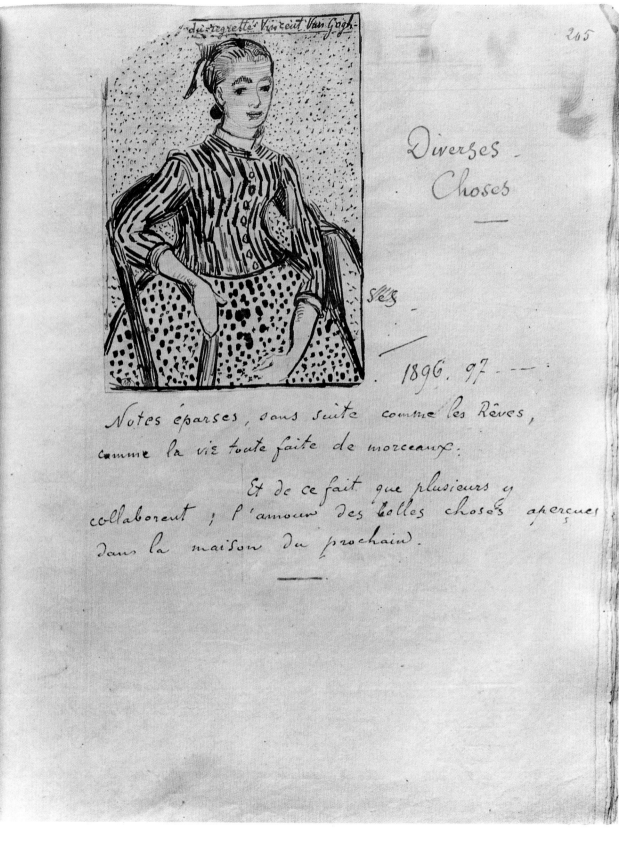

On this handwritten page by Paul Gauguin – entitled Diverses Choses *(Louvre Museum) –, the painter and friend of Van Gogh stuck a drawing of* La Mousmé, *headed with the words "From Vincent, who is sorely missed". Vincent painted the picture in Arles in July 1888, after reading* Madame Chrysantème *by Pierre Loti and before Gauguin moved into the yellow house.*

*Photograph of Doctor Paul
Gachet with a self-portrait of
Vincent Van Gogh. Doctor
Gachet, with Émile Bernard
and "Old Tanguy",
accompanied Theo to
Vincent's funeral at the
cemetery in Auvers-sur-Oise.*

On 29 July 1890 he died at one in the morning. "I would like to go home
now," were his last words.

In his study of the artist, Frank Elgar said: "Vincent could have become
a thinker, a poet, a hero, or a saint, just as he became a painter. Indeed,
we might think that he became all those things at once." One day he
decided to leave for his stars.

STILL LIFE, 1881
Oil on canvas, 44.5 x 57.5 cm
*Von der Heydt Museum,
Wuppertal*

STILL LIFE

1880 was a crucial year in Van Gogh's life. After going through a long period of inner struggle, he finally gave up his eager attempts to become a normal member of society and decided to live a Bohemian life and be a painter.

His fear of uselessness and loneliness gave way to a firm conviction that he wanted to be an artist. The same year he began to work as a professional painter and devoted himself to drawing as a form of personal resurrection: "In spite of everything I shall revive, take up my pencil, which I threw aside when I was so disheartened, and go ahead with my painting. From this moment everything seems to me to be transformed." When he took the decision everything changed: "I see things with different eyes than before I started to draw."

He started drawing with a Faber pencil, but replaced it with a rough carpenter's pencil, as he thought raw graphite was the material Dürer and Michaelangelo had used.

In December 1881 he began to paint in Anton Mauve's house in The Hague. Mauve was married to a cousin of his and was an established figure in the school of artists in the city. Mauve placed him in front of a still life with a pair of old clogs, a cabbage and some other elements. That was his first canvas and he immediately did the second, the one reproduced here. Both are dark and follow the line of traditional Realism; they maintain the forced rusticity that develops from the simplicity of form and the expressive strength which are characteristics of Mauve's paintings. His friend advised and corrected him and he made rapid progress, but the friendship was soon broken off. Vincent always felt gratitude towards his master: "I shall always remember my time in The Hague with emotion." When he left his cousin's house he had some oil paintings and a few watercolors.

The fact of beginning his professional career with these works conditioned the budding artist in two ways: the certainty that the still life was the basis of everything and a particular way of seeing things (flowers, corners of gardens, objects in his room) as if they were a still life. His predilection for this genre, which he treated assiduously in his first years as a painter, may have been influenced not only by a methodological and practical reason, but also by a commercial one: the genre was much in demand at the time and Van Gogh was searching resolutely for some form of income to prove to his family and his brother that he was capable of earning his own living.

Another factor which conditioned the painter at this early stage was his predilection for black and dark tones in the tradition of the Hague School. That was the subject of long arguments with his brother Theo, who had been influenced by the colorism of Parisian painting.

THE POTATO EATERS, 1885
Oil on canvas, 82 x 114 cm
*Van Gogh Museum (Vincent
van Gogh Foundation),
Amsterdam*

THE POTATO EATERS

Early in March 1885 Van
Gogh painted a small
canvas with four people
sitting at table in a humble
room in a cottage lit by the
light of a single oil lamp.
That was the first version
of the painting, now one of
the artist's best-known
works. He knew he was
going to paint an important
picture and made careful
preparations: since
February he had painted
thirty or so heads of
peasants and had done
other drawings at night.
After painting the first oil
he sent some rough
sketches to his brother

Theo and even a
lithograph for him to show
to the magazine *Le Chat
noir* to see if they would
publish it. He also tried
out the effect of the oil
with a gilded frame which
isolated it from the
surroundings at the house
of his friend Anton
Kersemakers and then he
did this final version.
This picture, the artist's
most complex in terms of
figures, is a perfect
summary of both his
technical conquests and
the inner feelings he had
experienced up to then. He
was coming to the end of a
long period of his life in
which his main obsession

had been to devote and sacrifice himself to his neighbor with an intensely religious concern. "I have tried to emphasize that those people eating their potatoes in the lamp-light have dug the earth with those very hands they put in the dish and so it speaks of manual labor and how they have honestly earned their food... And so I do not want anyone to find it beautiful or good." It was an indirect way of announcing the social meaning of the picture and his instinctive desire to share people's suffering. With this new, original composition Van Gogh was distancing himself from the path of Millet, though he would always nurture a sincere admiration for him. This picture also summarizes the technical ideas and theoretical foundations which sustained the artist at that time. "I am constantly in search of blue. The figures of the villagers here are almost always blue."

A blue which declares itself in broken, neutral tones in the exact way developed by Delacroix and the Ancients. In the end, it was a defence of shadows, of the subdued, neutral tones, of those colors "of which nobody knows the name and which are the basis of everything."

The work, which is roundly academic in approach, brought his Dutch period to a brilliant close. And in spite of the harsh criticisms he received, one of the most severe being from his friend the painter Anthon van Rappard, he wrote later to his sister Wilhelmina that it was the best thing he had done. And he told Rappard in reference to his criticism: "All that sometimes poisons my life and I think it quite possible that some people will feel sorry one day for what they have said to me and will regret having surrounded me with hostility and indifference."

THE VICARAGE AT NUENEN, 1885
Oil on canvas, 33 x 43 cm
*Van Gogh Museum (Vincent
van Gogh Foundation),
Amsterdam*

THE VICARAGE AT NUENEN

As in all Van Gogh's works, but in this one in a particular way, the artist's personal and emotional circumstances come together in the plastic values. This was the first time that the theme of a canvas had been so directly and personally linked to his life. The house in the painting is the family house where he spent nearly two years of his life. Then he rented an old sacristy because he thought that he would not be able to live with his mother and sister for any length of time, as he wrote in a letter to his brother: "...because of the distance between a person who wishes to keep up a certain social prestige and a peasant painter who is totally unconcerned with doing so... When I paint I am trying to find a way of living without preconceived ideas." That was freedom.
When Van Gogh went to live in the family house in Nuenen he set up his

studio in a wing built on in the garden. In the spring of 1884 Van Gogh did an accurately detailed drawing of the rectory from the garden, in which his studio can be seen between two trees. It was a documentary drawing. But in autumn 1885 he did a sketch of the vicarage face on, which he immediately transferred to oil. A little later he painted this canvas of the house in bright moonlight, repeating the composition of the drawing of 1884. We might wonder why he insisted on the theme at that time. We should remember that on 26 March 1885 Vincent's father died suddenly. From then on he worked intensively on *The Potato Eaters* as if to affirm himself in the face of his father's absence and he said: "The general impression was not terrible, just serious." From then on human figures gradually disappear from his painting and he concentrates on still lifes and empty landscapes. In one still life he placed his father's pipe and tobacco pouch. He painted another with his Bible open and beside it Emile Zola's *La Joie de vivre* (The Joy of Living), one of his own favorite novels. He painted a series of small oils with birds' nests, sometimes with eggs inside, and the old tower of the graveyard in Nuenen where his father was buried with the tombstones all around. His painting was turning to autobiography.

It seems that once his father had died, the artist was aware of his situation with the rest of his family and, apart from wanting to demonstrate that he had real qualities as a painter, he made an affective inventory of the places and objects which linked him to them. And in an allegorical reference, he painted empty nests: Nuenen was over. There were many reasons, from family ones to social ones. Vincent had too much desire for freedom to remain in that closed atmosphere. Moreover, he thought that he would not find new goals there: "Here I just paint tirelessly to learn how to paint." A situation which he described elsewhere: "I have to choose between a work place without work, here, and working without a work place, there." "There" was the future. And before he left he bequeathed us something of his life in his painting.

**"LA GUINGUETTE",
MONTMARTRE,** 1886
Oil on canvas, 49 x 64 cm
Musée d'Orsay, Paris

**"LA GUINGUETTE",
MONTMARTRE**

Van Gogh arrived in Paris
in March 1886, giving
Theo almost no advance
warning; he sent a brief
note which said: "Do not
be angry with me for
arriving unexpectedly.
I have thought about it a
great deal and there was
no point in wasting any
more time. I will be in the
Louvre from midday..."
He was in a hurry to see

classical painting and to
become part of the artistic
life of Paris. To immerse
himself in the new
atmosphere and work
towards a more luminous
style, he painted a long
series of still lifes in which
he tried out new colors and
tonalities.
As the theme for various
works he chose the popular
cafés and public places of
Montmartre, which were in
fashion at the time and
were painted by most of
the young artists. And so
in October 1886 he painted
La Guinguette (the
pleasure garden) of the
Moulin du Radet, known
as the Moulin de la Galette
and popularized on canvas
by Renoir and Toulouse-
Lautrec. Unlike them, who
reflected the gay, relaxed
atmosphere and the people
who went there, Van Gogh

concentrated on the simple garden where a few customers are drinking their glass of wine, because he wanted to reflect not the worldly, even refined, atmosphere, but the real life of the ordinary inhabitants of Montmartre. Simplicity and humility which harmonized with the preferences of his spirit nourished by the Realist novels of Zola.

Van Gogh painted three small oils of the mill with an identical composition, which capture the spot from the street. A photograph from the period allows us to see how, in spite of his fidelity to the model, Vincent sinks certain volumes so that the outline of the mill stands out against the sky.

A drawing, larger than the three oils, shows the inside: the small beer garden in the courtyard with the mill, the building at the entrance and the dance hall grouped around it. Vincent did the drawing with pen and pencil with touches of white lead and almost repeated the composition of the picture reproduced here; he just added, in the foreground on the left, the first steps of the wooden staircase leading up to the mill. The drawing must have been done in mid-winter because the trees are bare of leaves, while the brown leaves in the oil suggest that it was painted in autumn.

This canvas is one of the most important works of Van Gogh's Paris period. Its size shows that he

wanted to paint a major work and not a study to exercise different ways of combining color.

In the two years Vincent spent in Paris he painted about two hundred oils; most of them were studies in which he was impelled to experiment and to learn from the new theories and ideas his friends were developing.

As with *The Potato Eaters*, this canvas was not intended to be a study; he conceived and executed one of his masterpieces.

THE ITALIAN WOMAN
(AGOSTINA SEGATORI), 1887
Oil on canvas, 81 x 60 cm
Musée d'Orsay, Paris

THE ITALIAN WOMAN (AGOSTINA SEGATORI)

Agostina Segatori was Italian, born in the city of Ancona in 1841. She lived in Paris and was popular in artistic circles as she posed for a large number of painters. Van Gogh must have met her in January 1887 when she ran the Café du Tambourin. He fell in love with her and became a regular at the bar, though it was a spot that many people were wary of. Gauguin himself called it a thieves' den. Nonetheless, Vincent became a convinced advocate of the merits of the café and managed to attract a crowd of new customers: Anquetin, Bernard, Toulouse-Lautrec – who did a portrait of Vincent there –, Caran d'Ache, Steinlen, and Rollinat, among others. He even succeeded in getting Tanguy to come.

In the half year he was involved with Agostina, Van Gogh organized an exhibition of part of his collection of Japanese prints. He also hung his own work there, along with that of his friends. This friendship and sentimental relationship let Van Gogh to give her two still lifes with flowers, and

he painted two portraits of her. The first was done early in 1887 and it was conceived in a formula which was very much to the taste of the Impressionists: a woman sitting at a table alone, smoking, with a tankard of beer. Japanese prints can be seen on the wall. Towards the end of the year, when the intense relationship with Agostina had been broken off, Vincent did this portrait which everyone agrees is of her. It may have been painted from memory and she is presented as he really liked to portray people: looking more for a particular character, a type, rather than an individual. Hence the standard costume and the lack of precision in the features.

The compositional structure of the picture is very simple: a woman sitting facing the painter with her hands folded on her lap; on the left a strut and part of the back of the chair, the minimum required to indicate that she is sitting down; a plain background; in the upper right-hand segment a strip of perpendicular and horizontal lines; an orange line closes off the lower edge. The novelty of this work lies in its reduction of the sense of space, with a tendency towards flat painting in the style of the Japanese prints, which produces ambiguous effects. We do not know whether the woman is resting her hands on the material of the skirt or on another piece of cloth, on which two flowers which she is holding in her right hand are also resting. The brush strokes are rapid, short, and linear; the colors are complementary. Because of all those characteristics the work plays with the expressiveness of color, with impact. It was the first time that Van Gogh had expressed himself in this way, which was to become frequent in his Arles period.

Vincent recalled in a letter that Richepin had said: "Love of art makes us lose true love." And in this work and tribute, executed with passion from memory in recollection of someone he had loved, Van Gogh found the truest way for his art.

OLD TANGUY

Van Gogh painted four portraits of Julien Tanguy, known as "Old Tanguy". The first, an oil, was done in January 1887; the others, two oils and a drawing, at the end of the same year. Tanguy was a unique character. He sold paints from door to door to the artists of Montmartre until he opened a small shop in the Rue Clauzel. He was a Utopian socialist and an unconditional protector of the artists who could not afford to pay for his canvases and paints. In this way, his shop became the warehouse of the latest and most revolutionary painting and a meeting point for the newest and most revolutionary artists, who went to see their friends' works and discuss the theories that were being propounded in the world capital of art.

Van Gogh went to the shop in the Rue Clauzel, chatted to the shop-keeper and – took away the huge quantities of color he needed. There he met many artists, from Émile Bernard who became a close friend – to Paul Cézanne, with whom he discussed his theories and who told him, when he saw his portraits, still lifes and landscapes: "Frankly you paint like a madman." Van Gogh experts think that the two portraits of Tanguy done in autumn 1887 were painted in

OLD TANGUY, 1887
Oil on canvas, 92 x 73 cm
Musée Rodin, Paris

Bernard's new studio in Asnières and that the oil reproduced here must be considered the definitive version.

Tanguy is painted full face with his hands folded in his lap to make him look like a Buddhist monk, an impression reinforced by the background crowded with Japanese prints. Vincent had discovered Japanese art in Antwerp, where he started his collection of prints, which he added to considerably in Paris. The ones reproduced here, almost life size, were probably part of his collection. We do not know why he hung them as a background to the character in this portrait, as there is no evidence that Tanguy had any particular affection for them, but they were the most fashionable theme among the young artists who sought for ways to go beyond Impressionism with a new sense of color which they found in all forms of Japanese art. Vincent reinterpreted the prints and then treated the themes in his own manner, changing the original colors. He went beyond the light and color of the Japanese prints just as he went beyond Chevreul's optical theories made popular by the Impressionists. With a total lack of inhibition, he began to develop his innate sense of color, which bursts out of this

portrait. He had come a long way from the darkness of Holland and Belgium.

From this portrait he did a drawing on the back of a menu at the Restaurant du Chalet in the Avenue Clichy. It seems that he did not do that pencil portrait in the restaurant itself, but in his studio and, like the large oil painting, it is taken far from minutely detailed realism by the strength of the line.

SUNFLOWERS, 1887
Oil on canvas, 43 x 61 cm
*The Metropolitan Museum
of Art, New York*

SUNFLOWERS

Van Gogh is popularly
known as the painter of
sunflowers because of one
of his masterpieces, among
his most frequently
reproduced works. But it is
little known that the theme
of sunflowers had already
appeared while he was in
Paris. That was the period
when the artist wrote:
"I have painted a series of
color studies, simply
flowers: red poppies,
cornflowers, myosotis,
white and pink roses,
yellow chrysanthemums;
in search of the contrasts
of blue and orange, red and
green, yellow and violet, in
search of mixed, neutral

tones to harmonize the
brutality of extremes,
trying to find intense
colors and not a harmony
in gray. As we used to say,
'looking for life in color'.
True drawing consists of
modelling in color."
Shortly after writing that,
in the autumn of 1886 he
painted the first
sunflowers: a still life with
a vase full of different
flowers, among them roses
and sunflowers. The aim
of the deliberately
disordered bouquet was
not to reproduce particular
flowers but to create points
of color all intermingled.
Nonetheless, we can
recognize four sunflowers
among the group of roses.

In the summer of 1887 he
painted *Garden with
Sunflowers* in Montmartre.
But it was towards the end
of the summer when he
did four extremely
beautiful canvases:
sunflowers in outline on a
table. The theme of the
sunflowers was not one
discovered or imposed by
Vincent, since other artists
– among them Monet –
had already treated it. But
he was able to bring to it,
as to all his themes, a
special vision and force.
And so, because of the
unusual viewpoint from
which the composition is
established, these
sunflowers have been
compared to the series of

five nests he had done in Nuenen two years before. A comparison that cannot only be established in terms of form – where the parallels are obvious – but also in the symbolism of fertility, life, and nostalgia.

The two sunflowers in this work, one presented from the stalk and the other from the cup, are presented in the artist's customary style during his Paris period in a simple, violent contrast of complementary colors, blue and orange yellow. For Vincent this opposition of color had a well-defined connotation, as he had written: "Summer is to be found in full in the opposition of blues and the orange or golden bronze tones of the wheat."

With those words he has gone beyond the Impressionism-Pointillism on which he insisted so much in his Paris period and is embarking on the Symbolism and Expressionism which characterized his later periods.

**Self-Portrait
with Straw Hat,** 1887
Oil on canvas on wood,
35 x 27 cm
The Institute of Arts, Detroit

Self-Portrait
with Straw Hat

"I would like to paint the portrait of an artist friend who dreams big dreams, who works like the nightingale sings, because his nature is made that way. He will be fair-haired. And I would like to paint the esteem, the affection I feel for him. To begin with I shall paint him just as he is, that is, as faithfully as I can. But the picture will not be finished after that because to finish it I have decided to be an arbitrary colorist. I shall exaggerate the fairness of the hair... Instead of painting the mean, vulgar wall of the room behind him, I shall paint the infinite: I do a simple blue, the richest, the most intense I can prepare. And with that simple combination, the fair hair lit against that rich background produces a mysterious effect, like a star in the deep blue sky." Never has a painter expressed with greater feeling, with more of a sense of poetry, the conception of a work. Because he was not referring to a portrait of an unknown artist but, indirectly, to his self-portrait. In fact various self-portraits answer to that magical description. We only have to look at *Self-Portrait with Straw Hat* or *Self-Portrait at the Easel*, painted two or three months later, to realize that.

In the two years that the artist remained in Paris he did about twenty-three self-portraits and there are about ten more from the later periods, which also cover a good two years. It remains odd that the first picture the artist painted in Paris was also a self-portrait at an easel. But both works, quite parallel in composition, differ radically in their development of the concept of color. Van Gogh arrived in Paris exulting over the range of grays of a Franz Hals, whom he discovered in the museum in Amsterdam, and painted himself from that color scheme. But after the uninterrupted contact with the Impressionists and his friends, his ideas had changed completely. He

left the Académie Cormon, where Classicism was lauded as a mannered, academic formula, and practized all the concepts of color which he had rejected up to then: he had completely eliminated dark tonalities and gradually began to divide the tones. He followed the teaching of Pissarro, became infected by his friends and immersed himself in Japanese style. But he was never a painter of appearances, of the ephemeral, as the Impressionists are. And his personality led him to go beyond Impressionism. Hence the symbology of color. Hence what he called "canvases filled with meaning."

Johanna van Gogh-Bonger, Theo's wife, who met Vincent in May 1890, two months before the artist committed suicide, recalled him later as "a sturdy man with broad shoulders and a healthy complexion, a happy expression and an extremely determined bearing." But Vincent wrote to his sister Wilhelmina that at the time he had intended to show himself sad: it was the moment of disappointment with his life in Paris and nervousness about going to the south. This self-portrait, from the series he painted in the summer of 1887, no doubt shows that moment of the artist's inner struggle.

THE POSTMAN ROULIN

The person Van Gogh painted most insistently during his time in Arles – after himself – was Joseph Roulin. And not only him but also his wife and children on various occasions. Roulin was the postman in Arles, the only man in the South who understood Vincent. The artist was also attracted by the man's moral depth. "He is as revolutionary as Old Tanguy. He is probably considered a good revolutionary because he cordially detests... the republic we are enjoying." Roulin never wanted to be paid for posing. He was the man who took Vincent out of the brothel when he went to deliver the lobe of his ear to his friend Rachel and took him to his house. He managed to get Vincent out of the hospital where he had been interned on 1 January 1889. And, in the genius's first great crisis, he was by his side, until he was transferred to Marseilles on 21 January 1889.

Van Gogh was fascinated by his goodness: "Roulin is not old enough to be a father to me, but he possesses a silent dignity and feels a tenderness towards me of the kind an old soldier might feel for a young one." But he was also fascinated by his physical appearance: "He has a head like Socrates,

THE POSTMAN ROULIN, 1888
Oil on canvas, 81.2 x 65.3 cm
*Museum of Fine Arts (Gift of
Robert Treat Paine II), Boston*

almost no nose, a broad forehead, bald, small gray eyes, flushed cheeks, a splendid beard streaked with white up to his large ears." Van Gogh felt a strong attraction towards this character and needed him; his feelings about his friend led him to write: "I do not know if I can paint the postman as I feel him."

In late July 1888 he painted the first of the six portraits of him which he did in nine months. He painted him sitting, dressed in his navy blue uniform with the gold buttons. The background is also blue, the beard and the little that can be seen of the chair and a table on which he is resting his arm are green. In fact, Vincent was experimenting with a work in different tones of blue, wishing to emulate the works of Franz Hals which had so impressed him in Antwerp precisely because they were developed in a single range. Here the light and shadow of the suit, flecked with the gold of the buttons, are the most suggestive part of the work, which he did in a week. So we see that Arles freed him definitively from Impressionist theories and he returned to himself, to his innate and inevitable Expressionism. And he reached a maximum simplification.

From this work, Van

Gogh did two drawings: a rougher one to send to his friend Bernard and another, with touches of Chinese ink, for his brother Theo. It was his way of telling them what he was doing and how he was doing it.

In the drawing for his brother he added a glass, confirming the affectionate observation he had already made to him: "A Socratic type and no less Socratic for being somewhat alcoholic and thus rather flushed."

This portrait was the only one of Roulin almost full body; the other five are busts. One of them was done in a single, short session. Thus Vincent accomplished another of his most cherished aims: speed. He applied the paint in thick layers directly onto the canvas without any preparatory drawing. He gained speed, following the Japanese method: "They draw fast, very fast, like a flash of lightning; their nerves are finer, their feelings simpler." And he is aware of the risks: "You know I am in the midst of complex calculations, from which there emerge canvases, one after another, done rapidly, but calculated at length beforehand. And when people say they are done too fast, you can answer that they have looked too fast."

**THE CARAVANS, GYPSY
ENCAMPMENT
NEAR ARLES,** 1888
Oil on canvas, 45 x 51 cm
Musée d'Orsay, Paris

THE CARAVANS, GYPSY
ENCAMPMENT NEAR ARLES

Van Gogh's
humanitarianism must
have led him to plan this
gypsy encampment, as
they were a group of
people generally shunned
by society. In August 1888
we read in one of his letters
to his brother: "Then a
small study of a gypsy
resting place, red and green
caravans; and a small study
of carriages from the Paris-
Lyon-Mediterranean
express, and those last two
studies have been passed as
'very much on the modern
note' by the young disciple
of the valiant General
Boulanger, the brilliant

Zouave lieutenant."
Second lieutenant Paul-
Eugène Milliet once spent
some time with Van Gogh
in Arles. He was an art
lover – although he did not
like Vincent's work – , and
they took notes together
as they walked and talked
in the surroundings of the
town. Shortly after
painting this oil, Vincent
did his portrait. The soldier
recalled: "Sometimes he
set up the canvas and
started to daub. Then
everything went wrong.
That boy, who had a taste
and a talent for drawing,
turned into a crazy man
when he picked up a
brush." He approved of
this work because it was

outside the artist's usual themes.

In fact Vincent was looking for new subjects in Arles and he only found them – apart from the ones he took directly from his inner world – in carts and trains. He painted the Tarrascon stage-coach – influenced by reading Daudet –, gypsy caravans and railway carriages. The train was a theme Vincent returned to over and over again, incorporating it into his pictures as an element of contrast to the traditional life of the countryside. On this occasion he also depicted a tribe of gypsies with their caravans as a model of free life in direct contact with nature.

This work, of which Vincent did a pen and Chinese ink drawing, was painted very fast. Those were the days when he proclaimed the excellence of doing a portrait at a single sitting and, although he did not use his most brilliant colors, we find the transparency of the new air of the South. Those were also the days when he proclaimed the excellence of the sun and the light of that part of the world. With this unusual subject, Vincent celebrated a free, humble life, transparent air. "I am either lucid or blinded by love of work," he wrote at that time.

THE SUNFLOWERS

Van Gogh started to paint the Arles sunflower series to decorate his studio and have it ready for the arrival of his friend Gauguin. He knew that Gauguin liked the subject and although at first he thought of hanging the sunflowers in the studio, as a gesture to his friend he hung them in the guest room.

The project was to do a set of works on the same theme, one he was enthusiastic about. The enthusiasm stemmed from the imminent arrival of Gauguin, with whom he intended to start his artists' cooperative community project. Van Gogh's idea was to decorate the workshop with a dozen paintings of sunflowers, but he only painted four – with three, five, twelve and fourteen flowers – and of those he only considered that two were any good and signed them. Later he thought that those two works could form a triptych with *The Hand that Rocks the Cradle*, a retable with ideal motherhood as the central element.

For the artist those sunflowers were one of his most important works. Why? Because it was painted in a single range of color, yellow: a range of subtle hues with a few very fine lines of red and blue. He thought he had taken an important step in

THE SUNFLOWERS, 1888
Oil on canvas, 93 x 73 cm
The National Gallery, London

aspects of tone, similar to the ones taken by Vermeer of Delft. He told his brother: "To reach this high tone of yellow I have managed this summer, I have had to tear myself in two." He was so convinced of his efforts and achievements that he advised Theo: "You will see how these canvases catch the eye. But I advise you to keep them for yourself, for your intimacy with your wife. It is that kind of painting that changes appearance somewhat, that becomes richer if you look at it for a good while." That was why he selected the two pictures of sunflowers to present at the exhibition of the Salon des XX in Brussels in November 1889. Gauguin had always been fascinated by Vincent's sunflowers: he had two of the ones he had painted in Paris and had wanted to exchange them for the ones he did in Arles when he was staying in the yellow house, but Vincent considered them too good and did not want to make the exchange. But Gauguin, back in Paris, worked on Theo and, after some hesitation, Vincent decided to please him and made new copies, something which he always did with the canvases he considered his best. And so in January 1889 he made three "absolutely identical" copies. They were the ones that Gauguin obtained and one of them was the one which set an

historic record at an auction at Christie's in 1987.

"...but I own a bit of sunflower," Vincent said. So when Gauguin painted his friend's portrait he presented him painting a picture of sunflowers, which satisfied Vincent, who only rebuked him for having made him look like a madman.

SELF-PORTRAIT DEDICATED TO GAUGUIN

"I have specially bought a mirror which is good enough for me to work with my own face for lack of a model, because if I manage to paint the coloring of my own head, which is not without its difficulties, I can very well paint the heads of other good men and women," Vincent wrote shortly before painting this self-portrait. But the exercise was a cover for the fact that he could not afford to pay models and not a sign of exacerbated egocentricity.

In the self-portraits he did he almost never presents himself as a painter and he made a surprising variety of representations of his physiognomy. Perhaps because of that continuous introspection, scanning his own appearance and state of mind, painting his own portrait provided a strong motivation. On one occasion he roundly declared the primacy of portrait over landscape, not as a genre, but as his own practice: "I have a feeling of confidence when I do portraits, as I know that that type of work is by far the richest, though that is perhaps not exactly the right word; it might be better to say that it is what allows me to cultivate the best and most serious side of myself."

Van Gogh painted this

SELF-PORTRAIT DEDICATED TO GAUGUIN, 1888
Oil on canvas, 60.3 x 49.4 cm
The Fogg Art Museum, Harvard University Art Museums (Maurice Wertheim Collection), Cambridge

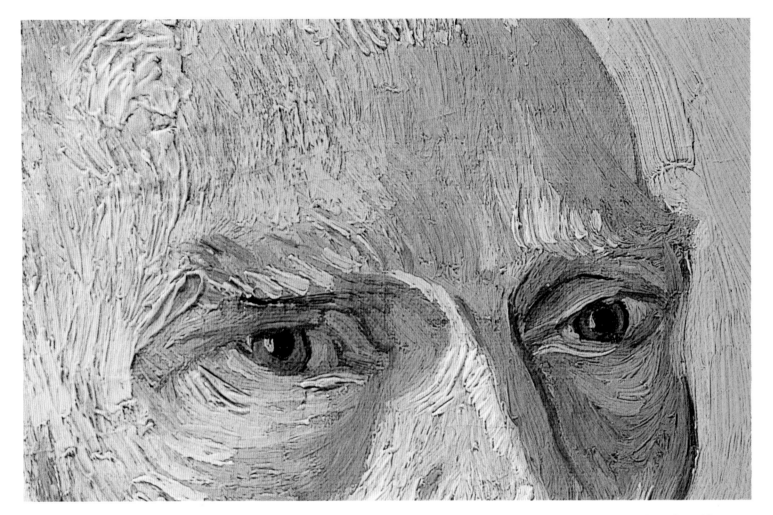

self-portrait in September 1888 and it bears a dedication: "To my friend Paul G." When the artist refers to it, he is talking about an almost colorless portrait with ashy tones on a pale green background on which he has put no yellow but has exaggerated the brown to purple and has bordered the jacket in blue. The head is outlined against a light background almost without shadows. But the outstanding feature of the work is that he has made his eyes slightly almond-shaped in Japanese style. That was not a result of the influence of the Japanese print, but a wish to please Gauguin. The story began when Van Gogh

suggested that Bernard should paint a portrait of Gauguin and Gauguin of Bernard. Portraits which he would exchange for works of his own and which would be hung to decorate the yellow house. In fact Vincent was laying a stratagem to put his two closest friends in touch so that they would encourage each other to travel south. But they did not paint one another's portraits; they did self-portraits in which they included a drawing of the other friend on the wall. In this self-portrait Vincent exaggerates his personality: "I have searched for the character of a simple monk adoring the eternal Buddha."

Here the artist achieves what he himself had said that only Rembrandt had managed to do, "tenderness in the gaze." For all that, this portrait is one of the most captivating he did.

THE YELLOW HOUSE IN ARLES, 1888
Oil on canvas, 79 x 94 cm
Van Gogh Museum (Vincent van Gogh Foundation), Amsterdam

THE YELLOW HOUSE IN ARLES

The centre of his activity in the Arles period, we know this little house inside and out from the paintings Van Gogh did of it and his descriptions in letters to his brother. There he spent perhaps his most crucial moment: his art found its fullest expression and his life reached a turning point as his psychological disturbance took a definitive turn for the worse. The artist himself called it the yellow house as he thought of decorating it with twelve canvases of yellow sunflowers. Yellow, his favourite color: "A light which, for want of a better word, can only be called yellow, pale sulphur yellow, golden lemon yellow. How beautiful yellow is!" The yellow house was to be the center of his community of artists in the South: a mixture of the Barbizon group and the Pre-Raphaelite Brotherhood or, in other words, a blend of religious and moral ideas to make real life easier to live and to share positions on art. But in the face of the impossibility of living with Gauguin and Vincent's psychological crisis, the project faded away.
He constructed this work with three zones of light: the foreground is yellow with green, reddish and pink hues. The center is yellow with zones of dark green, red and light green. The upper part, the sky, is

dark cobalt. The lightest yellow is the house. There is an inversion of the usual values in paintings, as the upper part is the darkest, which gives the lower part a greater luminosity. It is the embodiment of those Arles colors which had made such an impact on him and which he described to his brother in these words: "Here nature is extraordinarily beautiful. As a whole and part by part, the dome of the sky is an admirable blue, the sun has a glow of pale sulphur and is as soft and enchanting as the combination of the sky blues and yellows of Vermeer of Delft. I cannot paint anything as beautiful as that, but I am so absorbed that I let myself go and cease to think of rules."

Van Gogh does not often place figures in his works: here they are walking along the street with the viaducts and past the grocer's shop near his house and sitting on the terrace of the café. But in spite of that, the painting produces the same feeling of solitude as all the artist's works.

As on so many occasions, Van Gogh did a sketch in a letter so that his brother could have an idea of what it was like and see the colors of the new work. And, as usual, the differences in certain elements of the composition and in the intensity of the color itself were obvious.

The yellow house was where Vincent cut off his ear, and this got his name in the newspapers for the first time ever. In the local news section of *Le Forum républicain* of 30

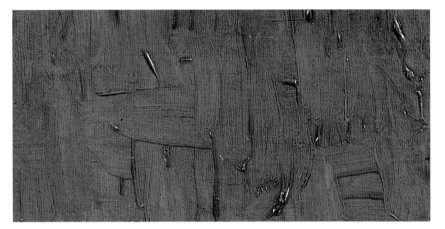

December 1888 the story read: "Last Sunday, at eleven thirty at night, a certain Vincent Van Gogh, a painter and native of Holland, appeared at brothel number one, asked for a certain Rachel and handed her his ear saying: 'Keep this safe.' Then he disappeared. Informed of the occurrence, which could only be the act of a poor, deranged person, the police went to his house the next morning and found him lying on his bed with almost no signs of life. The unfortunate individual was rushed into hospital."

When he came out of hospital he wrote to Gauguin, whom he so admired: "...until we have both had time to ponder the matter more deeply, do not speak badly of our poor little yellow house..."

VAN GOGH'S ROOM IN ARLES, 1889
Oil on canvas, 56.5 x 74 cm
Musée d'Orsay, Paris

VAN GOGH'S ROOM IN ARLES

Van Gogh painted this canvas two weeks after finishing *The Yellow House* as if he wanted to fix for ever the outer and inner appearance of his home. "Today I have got back to work. My eyes are still tired, but I had an idea in my head and this is the sketch. This time it is just my bedroom; just that the color has to predominate here, giving things a bigger style with its simplification and suggesting rest or sleep in general. In short, looking at the painting should rest the head or rather the imagination. The walls are pale violet. The floor is red squares. The wood of the bed and the chairs is a fresh butter yellow; the sheet and the pillows are very pale lemon. The bedspread is scarlet. The window green. The washstand is orange; the jug and basin blue. The doors lilac. And that is all, nothing more in this room with the shutter closed. The squareness of the furniture must emphasize the expression of a rest which cannot be interrupted. The portraits on the wall, a towel, a bottle and a few clothes. As there is no white in the picture, the frame will be white." Seldom has an artist given us such a precise account of a work, such a detailed description of all the elements which

excited at the imminent approach of Gauguin, for whom he felt a deep admiration and a latent sense of wariness and rivalry, and whose strength and protection he needed, while rejecting his security and success. Amidst those contradictions his bedroom had to convey a sensation of peace, of order, of a home which functioned normally. And he communicates that sensation. There is even a perceptible tender warmth in the austere arrangement of each piece of furniture and object. Perhaps because of the affection he felt when doing this work – not excluding the accomplishments with color, which reach the limits of a major work – Vincent considered it one of the most likeable and important pieces of his output.

Early in May 1889 Vincent sent the work to Paris for his brother to frame, but it had been seriously damaged and he sent it back to Arles for Vincent to copy before he had it restored. He immediately did a rather free version and, encouraged by the result, did a third, smaller one. He thought of giving that last one – the one reproduced here – to his mother and his sister Wilhelmina, to whom he wrote stressing the excellence of the color of the oil.

interplay in the composition. And, in turn, he gives us the key to the motif which inspired him to paint it: a feeling of rest, of repose, of tranquillity.

That feeling is basically what the painter was searching for at the time: to appear to be calm when deep down he was extremely anxious. As at other times of his life his feelings were in a state of turmoil. On the one hand, he had reasons to feel

cheerful: he was discovering new landscapes and a new light, which he records in an exalted and exultant manner; he thinks that he is near the start of his much desired and much discussed association of artists and he is making every possible effort for Gauguin and Bernard to come to the yellow house in Arles. But on the other hand, he is filled with unease, because he is still not selling his work; he is

L'ARLÉSIENNE (MADAME GINOUX), 1888
Oil on canvas, 93 x 74 cm
Musée d'Orsay, Paris

L'ARLÉSIENNE (MADAME GINOUX)

Van Gogh did few portraits during his stay in Arles because he had problems with his models, for both economic and personal reasons. But Gauguin knew how to be on good terms with people and persuaded Madame Ginoux to pose for them. Marie Ginoux was the owner of the restaurant where Van Gogh ate every day. One day she invited the two friends to have a coffee and they managed to get her to pose for them. Gauguin did a drawing and Vincent an oil which took less than an hour, in spite of the size of the format. Van Gogh was always attracted by the women of

Arles, the way they dressed and did themselves up. He declared: "I am not saying that they do not have beautiful figures, but that is not the local charm. Their charm lies in the magnificent cut of their clothes, their bright colors and the admirable way they wear them, in the tone of the skin rather than the figure." And so in this work he tried mainly to bring out the qualities of the garments: the shawl, the hair ribbon, the gloves on the table, all part of the typical outfit.

The friends must have sat one on each side of the model, as we can see from the works. Van Gogh held his friend's opinion in such esteem that he said: "Madame Ginoux, if Gauguin likes the picture your portrait will be in the Louvre in Paris." And he was not mistaken: Madame Goldschmidt-Rothschild presented it to the national museum the day after the liberation of Paris in 1944.

Van Gogh immediately did a second version of the work, certainly to give to the model, which was a usual form of payment among painters of slender means and models who were not in need of money. But in the second version Van Gogh changed the sunshade and gloves on the table for books. Although we do not know the real reason for the change, it has been interpreted as a wish to contrast the traditional character of the Provencal town with modernity epitomized by the two novels.

This work is different from the ones the Dutch artist was doing at the time because he uses flat forms, black as the dominant color and angular contours. Certain reminiscences of Japanese prints can be appreciated, but it would not be right to think that at that moment ideas he had left behind during his Paris period had come back to life in a particular work. It would be more logical to think of the influence of Gauguin, because of both his works and his theories. We are undoubtedly looking at a work of great beauty in the color, but it does not attain that unbridled dynamism and uncontainable force which are so characteristic of Vincent.

In late 1890, in Saint-Rémy, Van Gogh did five portraits of Madame Ginoux painted from the sketch Gauguin had done for him and which he had left in Arles when he departed. With that respect he felt for his friend, he wrote to Gauguin: "It is, we might say, the synthesis of a woman of Arles. And since syntheses of women of Arles are not so common, you must consider it a work by you and me, like a summary of the months we worked together."

VAN GOGH'S CHAIR

This is one of Van Gogh's best known pictures. In fact, between November 1888 and January 1889, he also painted *Gauguin's Chair*, which is an armchair to distinguish it from the other. It is most likely that the two canvases, which are practically the same size, were painted in November 1888, but Van Gogh put the finishing touches to his chair in January of the following year, while he never returned to the armchair.

Van Gogh introduces a new theme into the painting, the chair, and it is halfway between a still life and a Realist interior. It is true that chairs were one of the objects the students had to paint at art school to tackle the problem of perspective, but a chair had never been so radically the center of a work. Both canvases are extremely simple: the chairs on the bare floor with everyday objects on them: a pipe and some tobacco on Vincent's; a candlestick with a lighted candle and two books on Paul's. In the background of Vincent's, a crate with onions and a door; on the wall in the background of Paul's a gas jet alight. Simplification can go no further.

In spite of that, the two works are among the author's best known and those which allow us to come closest to an

VAN GOGH'S CHAIR, 1888
Oil on canvas, 46 x 38 cm
The National Gallery, London

understanding of Vincent's psychology. First, the chair is painted by day and the armchair by night. The chair may have come from the kitchen, though it is identical to the one Vincent had in his bedroom, and the armchair was in the guest room.

Vincent had described the two bedrooms in these words: "We shall have, as a guest room, the prettiest room on the top floor, which I would try to do up as well as possible, like the bedroom of a truly artistic woman. Then my bedroom, which I would like to be excessively simple, but with broad, square furniture: the bed, the chairs, the table, all white wood."

Although it is known that an empty chair popularly means absence or death, as in many places the chair where a dead person used to sit is often left unused, the interpretations of these two exceptional oil paintings are more complex, as complex as the artist's psychology. People have talked about Vincent's dependence on Paul, they have stressed his premonition that his friend would leave Arles; they have even related that dependence with the artist's feelings about his father and his latent homosexuality, which he tried to conceal by speaking of a woman when he thought of the person who would share the room in the yellow house with him.

Van Gogh had been impressed during his time in The Hague by a drawing of an empty chair done by Fildes and he looked for a reproduction

of the work, but failed to find one. Since then when he saw an empty chair he thought of death: "There are empty chairs everywhere and there will be still more; sooner or later there will be nothing but empty chairs."

**THE DANCE HALL
IN ARLES,** 1888
Oil on canvas, 65 x 81 cm
Musée d'Orsay, Paris

**THE DANCE HALL
IN ARLES**

Gauguin wrote: "That very evening we went to the café; he took a weak absinthe. Suddenly he flung the glass and its contents in my face. I dodged the missile and after I had restrained him, I left the café, crossed the square and, a few minutes later, Vincent was in bed where he stayed asleep until the next morning." In November and December 1888 Van Gogh's rhythm of life changed substantially with the presence of Gauguin: he wrote fewer letters to his brother Theo, to Bernard and his sister Wilhelmina; the references to his works are vaguer and, in many cases, he does not mention them at all. But the changes in his way of working are more important: he, who always painted from life, now began to paint from memory, basing his work on the emotions aroused in him by people and things, thus following Gauguin's theories. This process gave rise to works such as *Les Alyscamps, Autumn, Memory of the Garden in Etten, Spectators at the Arena in Arles* and to this canvas. Vincent was well aware of the change. One day he wrote: "Gauguin has made me vary my work a little." And to convince himself of the positive aspects of that: "Gauguin gives me the courage to imagine and

the things of the imagination have a more mysterious character." Thus when he explained *Memory of the Garden in Etten* to his sister Wilhelmina he told her that although there was no resemblance, the two figures in the picture could be her and his mother because "the color suggests the personality of the mother." That mental game of symbolisms and suggestions, of painting done from memory, exhausted Van Gogh. They argued. "The arguments spark excessive electricity. We sometimes go out with our heads like an electric battery that has run down." Hence the glass of absinthe flung in Gauguin's face was really

a gesture of rebellion. This canvas is an atypical work by Van Gogh, both in terms of the theme and the execution. Although he had spent two years in Paris, he had never painted the interior of a café-concert, so fashionable among young Parisian painters. And he paints it with compartmentalized color zones, as if it were a stained glass window, with lines marking out spaces, with spaces interwoven to form the composition. It is an atypical work because it follows a classical order and the restraint, balance, regulation, and subtlety propounded by Gauguin. For that reason it lacks intensity and expressive force. He returns to a human medium and feels

inhibited because he is feeling, temperament, vertigo, the dimension of dreams, curved lines, not straight ones. Gauguin made him imagine the composition, but restricted the development of the work; he starts from reality, but breaks all the rules when portraying it. The glass of absinthe thrown in Gauguin's face on 23 December 1888 was a protest against having done paintings like this one.

THE STARRY NIGHT, 1889
Oil on canvas, 73.7 x 92.1 cm
*The Museum of Modern Art
(Lillie P. Bliss Bequest),
New York*

THE STARRY NIGHT

"I confess I do not know why, but looking at the stars always makes me dream." That may have been why he had been unable to resist attempting night subjects for the last few years and in Arles he painted two extraordinary ones: *Night Café* and *Starry Night on the Rhône*, both in September 1888.

Nine months later, he painted this canvas, another of his major works. It was May and for almost a month he had been voluntarily interned in the sanatorium of Saint-Rémy-de-Provence, from where he wrote letters which are a mixture of tranquillity and tenderness, a desire to work and compassion for the other patients. He even talks about his depressions with the peace of mind of someone who is not a protagonist in spite of the acute crises he was going through. As a counterpoint, his canvases begin to show a new character, a logical consequence of his situation. This picture displays a dizzy

dynamism, an energy which had never appeared before, not only in his work but in the entire history of painting. As Karl Jaspers pointed out, the object gradually disappears as an individual thing, the notion of the particular dissolves until the whole picture becomes a whirlpool. It is as if he no longer wanted to describe, but to show a state of mind.

In Arles, when he painted the night with the candles around his hat, he said that he wanted to find "a way of trying out something calming, which would console us so that we no longer feel guilty or unfortunate." He though, that painting could be like music done with the emotion of a prayer. The notes of the oratorio were colors. "I have a terrible need for a religion. Then I go out at night to paint the stars." Now, in Saint-Rémy, he communes with nature directly and abandons himself to the infinite. His religious anxieties return, which makes him sad. For that reason his painting turns towards pantheism.

Van Gogh believed that he was painting this canvas in a way that would please Bernard and Gauguin, because basically it is more artificial, farther from his reality. Although he constructs with strong strokes, it is the zones of color that mark the composition. And he delves – it is night – into a sensation that is both brilliant and subdued. The stars look like suns. He does not want to shun yellow because before religious feeling he places the heat and color of the light he dreamed of for his yellow house, his home. Vincent was not satisfied with this work because he was never satisfied with the paintings which brought him close to Gauguin. But *The Starry Night* has remained as a unique landmark in the firmament known as Van Gogh.

**WHEAT FIELD
WITH CYPRESSES,** 1889
Oil on canvas, 72.5 x 91.5 cm
The National Gallery, London

**WHEAT FIELD
WITH CYPRESSES**

"Cypresses always attract me: I would like to do something like the sunflowers canvases, because I am surprised that nobody has done them as I see them yet," wrote Van Gogh in late June 1889. Van Gogh is renowned as the painter of sunflowers, but he should also be famous as the painter of cypresses. Nobody had done or could do them with his vigor and genius.

When he arrived in Arles he could not resist the impact of the light – the new yellow and the new blue – and succumbed to it; in Saint-Rémy he succumbed to the strength and the song of the cypresses. He was already seriously ill, but the tree revived his life impulses rising from the earth like a dark flame. He was already familiar with cypresses, but until that moment they had never called to his spirit. "It is the black stain on a landscape bathed in sunlight; but it is one of the most interesting black notes, one of the most difficult to capture exactly, that you can imagine." And with that calm simplicity with which he wrote at that time, he told Bernard: "My ambition is confined to a few clods of earth, the corn sprouting,

a cypress..."
It was "the black stain" on the landscape and he used that expression to refer to the human figure, and so he is not judging it from a purely plastic point of view, but endowing it with a humanized presence. It was no longer the simple vision of nature that made him react, but the spirit of nature. Spirit and essence which he communicates to us in an exceptional fragment from one of his letters in June 1889. "Outside the cicadas sing, shouting their heads off, ten times stronger than the crickets, and the burnt grass takes on beautiful tones of old gold. And the beautiful cities of the Midi are as dead as our cities along the Zuydersee, which used to be so lively. While with the fall and decline of things, the cicadas, admired by the good Socrates, endured. And here, indeed, they still sing in ancient Greek." It seems as though, as his mental crises worsen and his personal loneliness and isolation increase, he finds in nature what he has looked for in vain in men.

So much so that he even humanizes it, talking about trees as he did about people and speaking of the language of animals. It was shortly after entering the asylum of Saint-Paul-de-Mausole that he began to think about the theme of cypresses: *Green Wheat Field* was his first approach to the subject, on which he spent two months, leaving half a dozen works all quite different in concept, but all of unequalled value. As they were done at the same time as *The Starry Night* they are moving in the same direction, towards synthesis and a more abstract conception. The details gradually lose importance, there is a tendency towards a unified space, a single spatial meaning. A tendency towards a single idea.

**PORTRAIT
OF THE ARTIST,** 1889
Oil on canvas, 65 x 54 cm
Musée d'Orsay, Paris

PORTRAIT OF THE ARTIST

In August and September
1889, in the asylum of
Saint-Paul-de-Mausole, he
painted some portraits and
self-portraits. The last time
he had confronted his own
face was in January the
same year, while he was
still in Arles, his image
with the bandaged ear after
the final quarrel with
Gauguin. In that self-
portrait, staring into
emptiness, he left us his
last reference to the
Japanese prints: like a last
goodbye to his southern
dream: Arles was
his Japan.
He painted four other self-
portraits one after another.
Four images which
fulfilled the artist's
confessed desire: "I would
like to do portraits which,
in a century's time, people
would see as apparitions."

They are apparitions of a man whose profound gaze reveals the unfathomable abyss inside him.

In one of those self-portraits, almost certainly the first, he appears with a painter's palette in his hand and wearing his painter's smock, the first time he had depicted himself like that. He had just recovered from one of his attacks and was as thin and pale as a ghost. The picture is dark violet, his face whitish and his yellow hair and green beard give him a sickly look.

Later he painted two more in greens, blues and yellows, the last one unfinished, with his eyes deeper than in any other canvas.

The portrait reproduced here was painted after the first and is considered to be a continuation to show his state of health. Somewhat recovered, he began to work on this canvas and painted himself in a jacket and waistcoat, the most elegant appearance of any of his self-portraits. That was because he wanted to show his brother that he had recovered. In spite of his faith in his recovery and the therapy of painting, on occasions he even ate his paints and had to have an antidote administered, which explains his constant ups and downs, even at a time which might be described as stable.

When he described this work to his sister Wilhelmina, Van Gogh said that it was "a beautiful southern blue." The red of his beard and the green of his hair outline him and pick out the head from the rest of the work. Although he considered it a very good canvas, he did not make a reproduction or a water-color. Indeed, he thought it so good he considered that it was one of the paintings he originally thought of sending to the Salon des XX in Brussels, when Theo mentioned to him the possibility of exhibiting.

When he passed through Paris on his way to Auvers, Vincent collected the canvas from his brother's house and took it with him. "Monsieur Gachet (his doctor in Auvers) is mad about this portrait and wants me to make a copy for him, exactly the same, and I agree." But he did not do it.

THE HÔPITAL SAINT-PAUL IN SAINT-RÉMY-DE-PROVENCE

On 8 May 1889, Van Gogh was admitted to the hospital and asylum of Saint-Paul-de-Mausole in Saint-Rémy-de-Provence, where he remained until 16 May the following year. During his stay there his feelings about the hospital underwent a radical change. "When I saw the reality of the life of the madmen and other crazy people in that wild beasts' den, I lost that vague fear, fear of the thing. And little by little I came to consider madness as just another illness. Besides, contrary to what I expected, the change of atmosphere has done me good," he wrote early on. Some time later he said: "Within a few months I shall be so softened up and stupefied that a change will probably do me a lot of good. Although I do not feel capable of judging the way they have of treating the patients here, it is enough for me to see the terrible danger threatening what may remain of my reason and capacity to work." That change of feeling and sensation is reflected in the gradual distancing of the hospital as the centerpiece of his paintings. When he arrived he painted three gouaches of the atrium and corridor of the hospital and the window of his studio – Vincent had two rooms, a bedroom and a studio –, works which are exceptions in his production because he uses architectural themes. Afterwards he painted various canvases in the impressive, neglected

THE HÔPITAL SAINT-PAUL IN SAINT-RÉMY-DE-PROVENCE, 1889
Oil on canvas, 80 x 64.5 cm
Musée d'Orsay, Paris

garden of the center. One of them, *Undergrowth*, he presented at the Salon des Indépendants where Jo, Theo's wife, saw it and liked it so much that she kept it all her life. He also painted one of the rooms in the hospital with inmates and nuns – the omnipresent nuns, as the artist said – around a stove.

In October 1889 he painted the garden of the asylum on two occasions, including the facade of the large building which was constructed in the old priory of Saint-Paul-de-Mausole, parts of which dated from the 12th century. In spite of its size, the asylum was almost empty, with just fifteen inmates. There were three categories in the establishment and Vincent was installed in the third which was equivalent, as he said, to a restaurant with cockroaches in Paris. But he left us only a poetic vision of the place.

In the works which show the garden of the asylum of Saint-Paul-de-Mausole, Vincent consciously heightens his realism, moving away from the mystical painting of Gauguin. But he also delineated a certain idealism with the help of color and composition to give a vision of that tranquil place so full of life. Along that path he was guided by Delacroix, whom he admired so much. But he also wanted to establish metaphors about life and death, about the transitoriness and ephemerality of life. An anonymous man confronts a twisted tree – in this case – and an antiquated building. Man confronting nature and his own works.

THE SIESTA

"I want to be able to tell you what I am looking for in it and why it seemed to me useful to copy it. We painters are always required *to compose, to be nothing but composers*, and that is all very well, but in music it is not the same. And if someone plays Beethoven, he adds his own personal interpretation; in music, and especially in song, the *interpretation* of a composer is one thing and it does not have to be only the composer who plays his own composition." Vincent wrote that in mid September 1889 to justify the fact that he was making copies,

THE SIESTA, 1890
Oil on canvas, 73 x 91 cm
Musée d'Orsay, Paris

interpretations of different artists, especially Delacroix and Millet. By September 1889 he had already reinterpreted Delacroix's *Pietà* through a lithograph from Nanteuil. And from then on he made constant interpretations of the work of Millet, the passion of his life: peasants working in the fields, sowing, women spinning.

This insistence on a reinterpretation of the work of another artist may be justified by the fact that at the time Van Gogh did not have full freedom of movement, as he was shut up in the asylum of Saint-Rémy and the plates of his admired masters had to serve as models. That is a fact and it was basically the real reason why he did those works. But the text by Van Gogh reproduced here should not be considered a simple justification of his situation; it is an exposition of his peculiar way of understanding creation. Two other short texts shed more light on the subject. When the first article on his work signed by Albert Aurier appeared in *Le Mercure de France*, he felt very flattered and in his letter of thanks to the critic, in which he tells him that he is sending him one of the cypress works, he says: "It seems that things are attributed to me which would be better applied to Monticelli, to whom I owe so much. I also owe a great deal to Paul Gauguin, with whom I worked for a few months in Arles, and whom I already knew from Paris." From his deep socialist conviction, Vincent maintained a concept of shared creation, both in terms of the person who encouraged him to do the work and the one who established the composition. They all share the authorship of the work with the painter himself.

PRISONERS WALKING, 1890
Oil on canvas, 80 x 64 cm
Pushkin Museum, Moscow

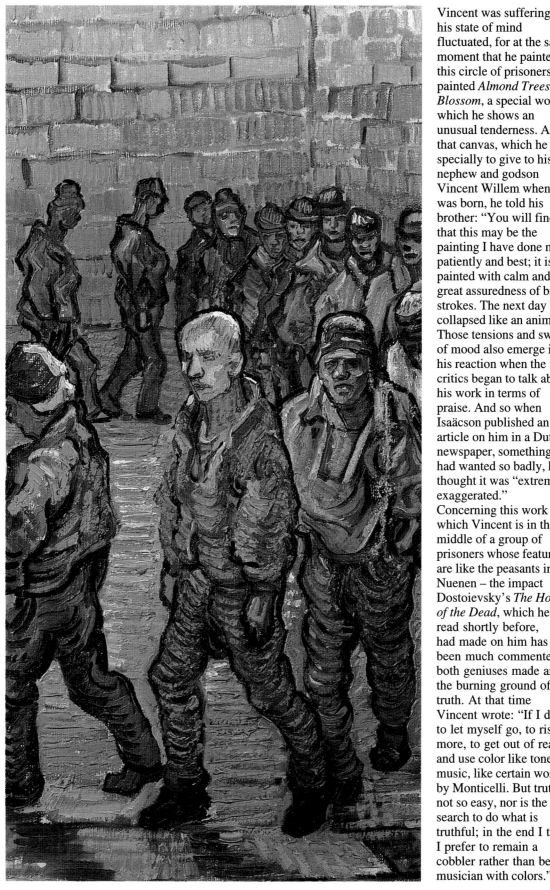

PRISONERS WALKING

This work was done by Van Gogh in February 1890 when he still had three months to go in the asylum in Saint-Rémy. It was the period of the reinterpretations of other painters, mainly Millet. He painted this oil from a woodcut by Gustave Doré who, in London in 1872, had published 174 plates to illustrate *London, a Pilgrimage*, by the now forgotten Blanchard Ferrold, who tried to reflect life in a modern city with its movements of crowds and social contrasts. Vincent discovered his work in 1877 and when he painted it he included himself in the circle of convicts. If we bear in mind that discovery and the choice of the work – the most disturbing in the whole volume – and we also think of the pathetic figure of the desperate old man in *On the Threshold of Eternity*, we must recognize the anguish that Vincent was suffering. But his state of mind fluctuated, for at the same moment that he painted this circle of prisoners he painted *Almond Trees in Blossom*, a special work in which he shows an unusual tenderness. About that canvas, which he did specially to give to his nephew and godson Vincent Willem when he was born, he told his brother: "You will find that this may be the painting I have done most patiently and best; it is painted with calm and great assuredness of brush strokes. The next day I collapsed like an animal." Those tensions and swings of mood also emerge in his reaction when the critics began to talk about his work in terms of praise. And so when Isaäcson published an article on him in a Dutch newspaper, something he had wanted so badly, he thought it was "extremely exaggerated."

Concerning this work – in which Vincent is in the middle of a group of prisoners whose features are like the peasants in Nuenen – the impact Dostoievsky's *The House of the Dead*, which he had read shortly before, had made on him has been much commented; both geniuses made art the burning ground of truth. At that time Vincent wrote: "If I dared to let myself go, to risk more, to get out of reality and use color like tones of music, like certain works by Monticelli. But truth is not so easy, nor is the search to do what is truthful; in the end I think I prefer to remain a cobbler rather than be a musician with colors."

DOCTOR GACHET'S GARDEN AT AUVERS-SUR-OISE, 1890
Oil on canvas, 73 x 51.5 cm
Musée d'Orsay, Paris.

DOCTOR GACHET'S GARDEN AT AUVERS-SUR-OISE

It seems that the first work he painted of the world of the doctor who was treating him, Paul Gachet, was this corner of his garden. He immediately painted portraits of him and his daughter in the garden.

In the Auvers period he painted this canvas and the garden of Daubigny, the artist he so admired, who had built himself a home nearby. From the first moment he was a regular visitor at the doctor's house, "...full of old black, black, black junk, except for a few Impressionist paintings...," where he had been recommended by Pissarro. He sometimes ate with the family and even during his last days he chatted at length with his host. The meals were a torture to Vincent, who called them abominable: for his stomach it was an absolute novelty to be fed five spicy dishes in quick succession.

If Daubigny's garden offers a broad panorama shut off by the artist's house and the buildings at the back, among them the famous village church, Doctor Gachet's was conceived with a foreground of vegetation with a glimpse of the countryside and a few buildings in the background. He no doubt wanted to use the cypresses in the garden, as they were few and far between in that landscape. The exoticism of the garden must have been attractive to Vincent: apart from his daughter Marguerite (also called Clementine) who was nineteen and her brother Paul, two years younger, the doctor enjoyed the company of eight cats, eight dogs, a goat, hens, rabbits, geese, pigeons, a tortoise, and a turkey. Thus the animal kingdom was blended with an interesting and highly varied collection of art and decorative objects.

Van Gogh portrayed Marguerite on two occasions: one playing the piano and another walking in the garden. That garden limited here to a foreground which, in its distorted perspective, breaks with the conventional laws of the vanishing point, raises the horizon, makes it disappear, bends the foreground and eliminates the middle ground.

THE CHURCH AT AUVERS

In the sixty-nine days that Van Gogh lived in Auvers he did eighty works. He painted at a frantic pace, which left him wrung out. In the last letter he wrote to his brother which was in his pocket when he shot himself in the stomach, he said: "I risk my life for my work and my reason is half destroyed..."

If we analyze the works Vincent left us over his life, we can see that he was never attracted by historic monuments. A few weeks after arriving in Arles he wrote to his brother: "There is a Gothic portal here which I am beginning to find admirable, the portico of Saint-Trophine. But it is so cruel, as monstrous as a Chinese nightmare, that even this beautiful monument of such a great style seems to me to be from another world to which I am as happy not to belong as to the glorious Rome of Nero." He might find them beautiful, but they did not move him, which is why they do not appear in his work.

Consequently the theme of this canvas of the church in Auvers is exceptional. He described the painting to his sister Wilhelmina in these words: "I have done a large picture of the village church, in which the construction looks violet against a deep blue

**THE CHURCH
AT AUVERS,** 1890
Oil on canvas, 94 x 74 cm
Musée d'Orsay, Paris

sky of pure cobalt; the windows look like stains of navy blue. In the foreground a little flowery green and pink sand. It is very similar to the studies of the tower of the graveyard I did in Nuenen, except that now the color is more lively, more sumptuous... It is true that the color is quite different, but that is not the only difference: the construction of the zones of color is done with short strokes in curved rhythms and earth and building seem to move, as if they were floating." That is the vibration which characterizes the artist's last period, when it was not just color – as in Arles – which defined the feelings, but also the composition.

DOCTOR PAUL GACHET, 1890
Oil on canvas, 68 x 57 cm
Musée d'Orsay, Paris

DOCTOR PAUL GACHET

It was Pissarro who told Theo that Vincent should move to Auvers-sur-Oise so that Doctor Gachet could look after him. He was a famous doctor in cultural circles in Paris and knew most of the artists; he had encouraged Cézanne to come to Auvers. He painted and bought works by the young painters when nobody else was buying them and he had exhibited under a pseudonym at the Salon des Indépendants. Van Gogh was in constant need of someone to stay by his side and help him and to confide in and in Auvers it was Doctor Gachet. They understood one another from the start, mainly on questions of art. But the doctor had a nude by Guillaumin which Vincent liked a great deal. He asked him to frame it to enhance the effect, but when he did not do so, Vincent was angry and provoked a quarrel which led to the first break between them. "I do not think I can count on Doctor Gachet at all. First he is sicker than I am, or at least as much as I am, so there is nothing more to be said. When the blind lead the blind, do they not both fall into the ditch?"

Vincent had been barely fifteen days in the small village, which had a long tradition as a place of residence for painters since Daubigny settled there, when he began work on the portrait of that eccentric character. With his white cap and his fair hair – the people in the village called him "yellow" – a blue jacket and a cobalt blue background of hills, he is leaning his hand on a red table where there are two yellow books and a plant in a vase with purple flowers. "It is in the same line of feeling as my portrait, which I brought when I came here." (Vincent was referring to the self-portrait in blue and green he did in Saint-Rémy). The doctor was fired with enthusiasm for the work and *L'Arlésienne*, which the artist kept in his room. Van Gogh never tried to paint realistic portraits, but to express the emotion of the moment. Here he wanted to reflect "the distressed visage of our age". As usual, he gave the model the portrait and made a copy for himself, eliminating the books and the vase – the version reproduced here – and, unusually for him, did an engraving from the second version with notable differences and printed it on the press that Gachet had in his house.

**HOUSES WITH THATCHED
ROOFS, CORDEVILLE,** 1890
Oil on canvas, 73 x 92 cm
Musée d'Orsay, Paris

HOUSES WITH THATCHED ROOFS, CORDEVILLE

When Vincent was still in Saint-Rémy he had expressed a wish to do a series of works with cottages and peasants, returning to the themes of his time in Brabant. He asked his family to send him his old sketches to do new works which would be memories of the north, but the project never came to fruition.
Once he had settled in Auvers he found a landscape which offered him artistic themes which had been worked by numerous artists and were already classics in French painting. But Van Gogh was inclined not towards the coldness of a Pissarro, a Cézanne or a Guillaumin, but to the expressiveness of Daubigny. He had told Bernard that what he most admired was the primitive "...hut with its mossy thatched roof and its sooty chimney." Auvers provided these houses and cottages with thatched roofs which were really within the tradition of the conventional picturesque which he painted in Brabant and Drenthe and even at Saintes-Maries-de-la-Mer on the brief excursion he made from Arles. In a letter to Bernard he had written: "Ah! If only one could know things as they used to be and paint the people who lived in those houses, it would be as pretty as a picture by Millet; but I am not referring to color, but

to the spirit, to something with meaning, to something to believe in." From his time in Auvers he left us a number of houses and cottages which capture that spirit. The houses with their thatched roofs on the outskirts of Cordeville, a small hamlet, are presented fully integrated into the landscape, with no strident color, very elaborately conceived and composed, the volumes set side by side with great skill. We cannot ignore the fact that he returned to the themes of his artistic youth, which were more linked with ethical and religious aspects than plastic ones. In Van Gogh there is always an underlying attraction towards neglected and helpless people which he justified in this last period with artistic arguments. But in the end that inclination for huts was more a revival of old feelings than a return to old themes, although he declared that his true religion at that time was work, his work: painting.

ROSES AND ANEMONES, 1890
Oil on canvas, 51 x 51 cm
Musée d'Orsay, Paris

ROSES AND ANEMONES

The period from *Still Life with Cabbage* to the canvas reproduced here covers almost the entire production of Van Gogh, as this last vase of flowers was painted in June 1890, a month before his suicide: the beginning and end of ten years' work with the constant, abundant presence of still lifes, especially flower themes.

Van Gogh always worked on flower paintings when he was worried about money: he thought that they were easier to sell, though his pictures with flowers did not sell either. As well as being a commercial resource to solve his financial problems with models and avoid his inevitably complex relations with them, the pictures with flowers motivated Vincent to try out contrasts and ranges of color. And so in the sun flower canvases he used matching tones; in *Still Life with Lilies* – painted a month before in Saint-Rémy – he posed the contrast of complementary colors. In this work, as in others done at the time – *Still Life with Hollyhocks* – he is searching for contrasts between reds, yellows, and greens. This work – the last or last but one still life with flowers he painted – presents a rose drooping to the right, a somewhat faded bloom. It was a compositional resource that Vincent used on more than one occasion, as in the work with lilies we have mentioned. A resource to balance the composition, which he

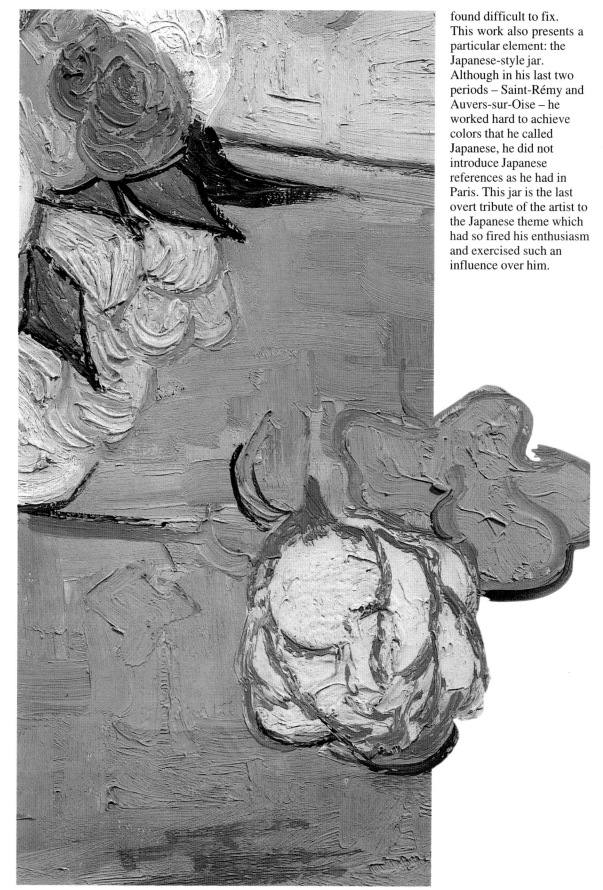

found difficult to fix. This work also presents a particular element: the Japanese-style jar. Although in his last two periods – Saint-Rémy and Auvers-sur-Oise – he worked hard to achieve colors that he called Japanese, he did not introduce Japanese references as he had in Paris. This jar is the last overt tribute of the artist to the Japanese theme which had so fired his enthusiasm and exercised such an influence over him.

Two Sulky Children, 1890
Oil on canvas, 51,2 x 51 cm
Musée d'Orsay, Paris

TWO SULKY CHILDREN

We know nothing about these two children that Van Gogh painted in June 1890 and whom he does not even mention in his letters. He painted them twice: once sulky, once smiling, in the same pose and against the same background.

Van Gogh seldom painted children. In his Arles period he did portraits of Joseph Roulin's children: Camille, who was still a boy, and Marcelle, who was still a baby. He painted her on two occasions. In Saint-Rémy he did not paint any children, but it should be pointed out that some of the prints he copied were on the theme of children: thus *Woman with Child on her Lap* taken from a reproduction of *The Husband is Away at Sea* by Virginie Demont-Breton; or *Peasants' House with Child in the Cradle*, taken from the series *The Four Hours of the Day* by Millet; or *First Steps*, also from a work by Millet. Those works have their justification: his sister-in-law was expecting a baby, which caused Vincent some concern over the expenses his brother would incur and perhaps over whether it would affect him. If he seemed to be anxious and rejecting the new arrival in his letters, in the works he showed interest in subjects of children and the treatment was even tender. This work has been considered on occasions as "extremely unfortunate", but it is clearly a sample of the Auvers period; it was done in a very short time and the nervousness of the strokes betrays extreme agitation. Karl Jaspers said that this elemental vehemence imposed monotony by eliminating all individual reference; earth, vegetation, and people have the same connotations of chaos. Nevertheless, the bold strokes of color mark out the theme with a strength which has rarely been equalled.

**WHEAT FIELD
WITH CROWS,** 1890
Oil on canvas,
50.5 x 100.5 cm
*Van Gogh Museum
(Vincent van Gogh
Foundation), Amsterdam*

WHEAT FIELD WITH CROWS

This canvas is one of Van Gogh's mystical paintings and is often supposed to be his last, though in fact it was only one of the last. It is part of a group of canvases painted in Auvers on the theme of the harvest: some show fields of corn; others fields recently reaped with the sheaves; others, pale fields stripped of their fruit. In the last letter Vincent sent his bother Theo he included two sketches "which show cornfields after the rain."
It was not the first time that Van Gogh had painted the theme: in Paris he had done a *Wheat Field with Lark*. It has been said repeatedly that in these works Vincent was making a paraphrase of the fields done by Georges Michel; like no other painter he achieved a sense of depth, a total skill for penetrating surfaces and communicating distances. He had a vision of the promised land, a threshold of immensity which his short life prevented him from developing in all its possibilities. From his time in The Hague, Vincent knew Michel's work and his aspirations. But if we compare both works, Van Gogh's has the greater spontaneity, the greater audacity and vigor. Vincent's fields with stormy skies have been interpreted as works which foreshadow his death. While he was painting them the tone of his letters was really somber. His state of mind was "... almost too great a serenity, the right state of mind to paint this". And he confessed that in them – although he had attempted it before with other works – he wanted "to try to express their extreme sadness and loneliness." A sadness and loneliness that weighed on him those days because in the face of Theo's economic problems, he feared, in spite of the protestations of his sister-in-law Jo, that his brother would stop helping him.
He transferred the melancholy and anguish which gripped him inwardly with total precision to these solitary fields flocked with crows, with roads leading nowhere, with dark skies and the sea of corn which looks like an overwhelming wave – powerlessness in the face of immensity.

VAN GOGH

THE COMPLETE WORKS

WORKS

1 • Still Life with Cabbage and Clogs, 1881
Oil on paper on panel, 34.5 x 55 cm
Van Gogh Museum, Amsterdam

2 • Still Life, 1881
Oil on canvas, 44.5 x 57.5 cm
Von der Heydt Museum, Wuppertal

3 • Cluster of Old Houses with the New Church in The Hague, 1882
Oil on canvas on cardboard, 35 x 25 cm

4 • Lying Cow, 1882
Oil on canvas, 30 x 50 cm

5 • Beach at Scheveningen in Calm Weather, 1882
Oil on paper on panel, 35.5 x 49.5 cm
Van Ogtrop-Van Kempen Collection, Aalst-Waalare

6 • Beach at Scheveningen in Stormy Weather, 1882
Oil on paper on cardboard, 34.5 x 51 cm
Stedelijk Museum, Amsterdam

7 • Women Mending Nets in the Dunes, 1882
Oil on paper on panel, 42 x 62.5 cm
Private Collection

8 • Dunes, 1882
Oil on panel, 36 x 58.5 cm
Private Collection

9 • Dunes with Figures, 1882
Oil on canvas on panel, 24 x 32 cm
Hahnloser Collection, Bern

10 • Two Women in the Woods, 1882
Oil on paper on panel, 31 x 24.5 cm
Private Collection

11 • Girl in the Woods, 1882
Oil on panel, 35 x 47 cm
Private Collection

12 • Girl in White in the Woods, 1882
Oil on canvas, 39 x 59 cm
Rijksmuseum Kröller-Müller, Otterlo

13 • Edge of a Wood, 1882
Oil on canvas on panel, 34.5 x 49 cm
Rijksmuseum Kröller-Müller, Otterlo

14 • Bulb Fields, 1883
Oil on canvas on cardboard, 48 x 65 cm
National Gallery of Art, Washington

15 • Cows in the Meadow, 1883
Oil on canvas on panel, 31.5 x 44 cm
Private Collection

16 • A Girl in the Street, Two Coaches in the Background, 1883
Oil on canvas on panel, 42 x 53 cm
Jäggli-Hahnloser Collection, Winterthur

1

2

3

4

5

6

7

8

9

10

11

12

13

14

15

16

17

18

19

20

21

22

23

24

25

26

27

28

29

30

31

32

17 • **A Windblown Tree, 1883**
Oil on canvas, 35 x 47 cm

18 • **Potato Digging, 1883**
Oil on canvas, 39.5 x 94.5 cm
Julian J. Raskin Collection, New York

19 • **Fisherman on the Beach, 1883**
Oil on canvas on panel, 51 x 33.5 cm
Rijksmuseum Kröller-Müller, Otterlo

20 • **Fisherman's Wife
on the Beach, 1883**
Oil on canvas on panel, 52 x 34 cm
Rijksmuseum Kröller-Müller, Otterlo

21 • **Footbridge Across a Ditch, 1883**
Oil on canvas on panel, 46 x 34 cm
Private Collection

22 • **Landscape with Dunes, 1883**
Oil on panel, 33.5 x 48.5 cm
Private Collection

23 • **Farmhouses in Loosduinen
Near The Hague at Twilight, 1883**
Oil on canvas on panel, 33 x 50 cm
*Centraal Museum (on loan from
the van Baaren Museum), Utrecht*

24 • **Farmhouses Among Trees, 1883**
Oil on canvas on panel, 29 x 39 cm
Private Collection

25 • **Farmhouses, 1883**
Oil on canvas, 36 x 55.5 cm
Van Gogh Museum, Amsterdam

26 • **Man Digging, 1882-1883**
Oil on paper on panel, 31 x 29.5 cm
Private Collection

27 • **Two Peasant Women
in a Peat Field, 1883**
Oil on canvas, 27.5 x 36.5 cm
Van Gogh Museum, Amsterdam

28 • **Peat Boat with Two Figures, 1883**
Oil on canvas on panel, 37 x 55.5 cm
Private Collection

29 • **Peasant Burning Weeds, 1883**
Oil on panel, 30.5 x 39.5 cm
Private Collection

30 • **Landscape with a Church
at Twilight, 1883**
Oil on cardboard on panel, 35 x 52 cm
Private Collection

31 • **Farmhouse with Peat Stacks, 1883**
Oil on canvas, 37.5 x 55.5 cm
Van Gogh Museum, Amsterdam

32 • **Chapel at Nuenen
with Churchgoers, 1884**
Oil on canvas, 41 x 32 cm
Van Gogh Museum, Amsterdam

WORKS

33 • Weaver Facing Right, 1884
Oil on canvas, 48 x 46 cm
Hahnloser Collection, Bern

34 • Weaver Facing Right, 1884
Oil on canvas, 37 x 45 cm
Private Collection

**35 • The Old Tower of Nuenen
with People Walking, 1884**
Oil on canvas on panel, 33.5 x 44 cm
Private Collection

**36 • The Old Tower of Nuenen
with a Ploughman, 1884**
Oil on canvas, 34.5 x 42 cm
Rijksmuseum Kröller-Müller, Otterlo

**37 • Weaver Facing Left,
with Spinning Wheel, 1884**
Oil on canvas, 61 x 85 cm
Museum of Fine Arts, Boston

38 • Peasant Spinning, 1884
Gouache on paper, 33 x 44 cm
Wildenstein Collection, New York

**39 • Landscape with Pollard
Willows, 1884**
Oil on canvas on panel, 43 x 58 cm

40 • Weaver Arranging Threads, 1884
Oil on canvas on panel, 41 x 57 cm
Rijksmuseum Kröller-Müller, Otterlo

41 • Weaver Arranging Threads, 1884
Oil on panel, 19 x 41 cm
Private Collection

**42 • The Old Church Tower
at Nuenen, 1884**
Oil on canvas on panel, 47.5 x 55 cm
Bührle Collection, Zurich

**43 • Water Mill at Kollen
Near Nuenen, 1884**
Oil on canvas on cardboard,
57.5 x 78 cm
Private Collection

44 • Village at Sunset, 1884
Oil on canvas on cardboard, 57 x 82 cm
Van Gogh Museum, Amsterdam

**45 • Weaver Standing in Front
of a Loom, 1884**
Oil on canvas, 55 x 79 cm
Private Collection

**46 • Weaver, Seen from
the Front, 1884**
Oil on canvas, 70 x 85 cm
Rijksmuseum Kröller-Müller, Otterlo

**47 • Weaver, Interior with
Three Small Windows, 1884**
Oil on canvas, 61 x 93 cm
Rijksmuseum Kröller-Müller, Otterlo

**48 • Weaver Near an
Open Window, 1884**
Oil on canvas on cardboard,
68.5 x 93 cm
*Bayerische Staatsgemäldesammlungen,
Munich*

33

34

35

36

37

38

39

40

41

42

43

44

45

46

47

48

49

50

51

52

53

54

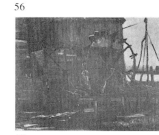

55

56

57

58

59

60

61

62

63

64

49 • Weaver, Seen from the Front, 1884
Oil on canvas on panel, 48 x 61 cm
Museum Boymans-van Beuningen, Rotterdam

50 • Cart with Red and White Ox, 1884
Oil on canvas on panel, 57 x 82.5 cm
Rijksmuseum Kröller-Müller, Otterlo

51 • Cart with Black Ox, 1884
Oil on canvas, 60 x 80 cm
Private Collection

52 • The Old Tower in the Fields, 1884
Oil on canvas on cardboard, 35 x 47 cm
Private Collection

53 • Farmers Planting Potatoes, 1884
Oil on canvas, 66 x 149 cm
Rijksmuseum Kröller-Müller, Otterlo

54 • Potato Planting, 1884
Oil on canvas, 70.5 x 170 cm
Von der Heydt Museum, Wuppertal

55 • Wood Gatherers in the Snow, 1884
Oil on canvas on panel, 67 x 126 cm
Private Collection

56 • Avenue of Poplars in Autumn, 1884
Oil on canvas on panel, 98.5 x 66 cm
Van Gogh Museum, Amsterdam

57 • Water Mill at Gennep, 1884
Oil on cardboard, 75 x 100 cm
Private Collection

58 • Water Mill at Gennep, 1884
Oil on canvas on cardboard, 87 x 151 cm

59 • Water Mill at Gennep, 1884
Oil on canvas, 60 x 78.5 cm
Rijksbureau voor Beeldende Kunst, The Hague

60 • Head of a Peasant with a Pipe, 1885
Oil on canvas, 44 x 32 cm
Rijksmuseum Kröller-Müller, Otterlo

61 • Still Life with Coffee Mill, Pipe Case, and Jug, 1884
Oil on canvas, 34 x 43 cm
Rijksmuseum Kröller-Müller, Otterlo

62 • Still Life with Pottery and Two Bottles, 1884
Oil on canvas, 40 x 56 cm
Private Collection

63 • Still Life with Clogs and Pots, 1884
Oil on canvas on panel, 42 x 54 cm
Centraal Museum (on loan from the van Baaren Museum), Utrecht

64 • Head of a Peasant Woman with Dark Cap, 1884
Oil on canvas on panel, 35 x 26 cm
Private Collection

**65 • Head of a Peasant Woman
with White Cap, 1884**
Oil on canvas on panel, 42.5 x 34 cm
Van Gogh Museum, Amsterdam

**66 • Head of a Peasant Woman
with Dark Cap, 1884-1885**
Oil on canvas on panel, 37.5 x 24.5 cm
Art Museum, Cincinnati

**67 • Head of a Peasant Woman
with Dark Cap, 1884-1885**
Oil on canvas on panel, 40 x 30 cm

68 • Peasant Woman, Head, 1884
Oil on canvas on panel, 47.5 x 34.5 cm
Van Gogh Museum, Amsterdam

**69 • Head of a Peasant Woman
with White Cap, 1884**
Oil on canvas, 43.5 x 37 cm
Private Collection

**70 • Peasant Woman, Seated,
with White Cap, 1884**
Oil on canvas on panel, 36 x 26 cm
Wirth Collection, Basel

**71 • Head of a Peasant Woman
with Dark Cap, 1884-1885**
Oil on canvas on panel, 25 x 19 cm
Private Collection

**72 • Head of a Peasant Woman
with Dark Cap, 1884**
Oil on canvas, 38.5 x 26.5 cm
Musée d'Orsay, Paris

**73 • The Vicarage Garden
at Nuenen, 1884**
Oil on paper on panel, 27 x 57 cm
Groninger Museum, Groningue

**74 • Still Life with Three
Beer Mugs, 1884**
Oil on canvas on cardboard, 32 x 43 cm
Van Gogh Museum, Amsterdam

**75 • Still Life with Four Stone
Bottles, Flask, and White Cup, 1884**
Oil on canvas, 33 x 41 cm
Rijksmuseum Kröller-Müller, Otterlo

76 • Still Life with Five Bottles, 1884
Oil on canvas, 46.5 x 56 cm
Bremmer Collection, The Hague

**77 • Still Life with Pottery,
Bottles, and a Box, 1884**
Oil on canvas on cardboard, 31 x 42 cm
Van Gogh Museum, Amsterdam

**78 • Still Life with Two Sacks
and a Bottle, 1884**
Oil on canvas on panel, 30.5 x 41 cm
Bremmer Collection, The Hague

**79 • Still Life with Pottery,
Beer Glass, and Bottle, 1884-1885**
Oil on canvas on panel, 31 x 41 cm
Private Collection

**80 • Still Life with Pots,
Jar, and Bottles, 1884**
Oil on canvas, 29.5 x 39.5 cm
Haags Gemeentemuseum, The Hague

65

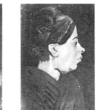
66

67

68

69

70

71

72

73

74

75

76

77

78

79

80

81

82

83

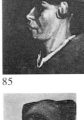

84

85

86

87

88

89

90

91

92

93

94

95

96

81 • Still Life with Three Bottles and Earthenware Vessel, 1884-1885
Oil on canvas, 39.5 x 56 cm
Van Gogh Museum, Amsterdam

82 • Head of a Peasant Woman with White Cap, 1885
Oil on canvas on panel, 41 x 31.5 cm
Bührle Collection, Zurich

83 • The Old Station at Eindhoven, 1884-1885
Oil on canvas, 15 x 26 cm

84 • Head of a Peasant Woman with Cap, 1884-1885
Oil on canvas, 42 x 35 cm
Van Gogh Museum, Amsterdam

85 • Head of a Peasant Woman, 1884-1885
Oil on canvas on panel, 40 x 32.5 cm
Private Collection

86 • Head of a Young Peasant Woman with Dark Cap, 1884-1885
Oil on canvas, 39 x 26 cm
Rijksmuseum Kröller-Müller, Otterlo

87 • Head of a Peasant, 1884-1885
Oil on canvas, 47 x 30 cm
Rijksmuseum Kröller-Müller, Otterlo

88 • Head of a Peasant Woman with Dark Cap, 1884-1885
Oil on canvas on panel, 39.5 x 30 cm
Private Collection

89 • Head of a Brabant Peasant Woman with Dark Cap, 1884-1885
Oil on canvas on panel, 26 x 20 cm
Rijksmuseum Kröller-Müller, Otterlo

90 • Head of a Peasant Woman with White Cap, 1884-1885
Oil on canvas on panel, 40.5 x 30.5 cm
O. Hosner Collection, Montreal

91 • Head of Peasant Woman with Dark Cap, 1884-1885
Oil on canvas, 32 x 24.5 cm
Private Collection

92 • Head of a Peasant Woman with Brownish Cap, 1884-1885
Oil on canvas, 40 x 30 cm
Rijksmuseum Kröller-Müller, Otterlo

93 • Head of a Peasant Woman with Dark Cap, 1885
Oil on canvas, 40 x 30.5 cm

94 • Head of an Old Peasant Woman with Dark Cap, 1884-1885
Oil on canvas, 36 x 25.5 cm
Rijksmuseum Kröller-Müller, Otterlo

95 • Peasant Woman, Seated with White Cap, 1884-1885
Oil on paper on panel, 40.6 x 31.7 cm
Noordbrabants Museum, Herzogenbusch

96 • Head of a Peasant Woman with Dark Cap, 1885
Oil on canvas on panel, 40.6 x 31.7 cm
Private Collection

97 • Peasant Woman, Seated, 1885
Oil on canvas on panel, 45 x 27 cm
Private Collection

98 • Two Hands, 1885
Oil on canvas on panel, 29.5 x 19 cm
Private Collection

**99 • The Old Cemetery Tower
at Nuenen in the Snow, 1885**
Oil on canvas on cardboard, 30 x 41.5 cm
Niarchos Collection, Athens

**100 • The Vicarage Garden
at Nuenen in the Snow, 1885**
Oil on canvas on panel, 51 x 77 cm
*Norton Simon Museum of Art,
Passadena*

**101 • The Vicarage Garden at
Nuenen in the Snow, 1885**
Oil on canvas on panel, 53 x 78 cm
*The Armand Hammer Museum of Art,
Los Angeles*

**102 • Head of a Young Peasant
in a Peaked Cap, 1885**
Oil on panel, 44.5 x 33.5 cm
*The Nelson-Atkins Museum of Fine
Art, Kansas City*

**103 • Head of a Peasant
with Cap, 1885**
Oil on canvas, 33.5 x 26 cm
Niarchos Collection, Athens

104 • Peasant Making a Basket, 1885
Oil on canvas, 41 x 35 cm
Private Collection

**105 • Head of a Peasant Woman
with Dark Cap, 1885**
Oil on canvas, 43.5 x 30 cm
Van Gogh Museum, Amsterdam

**106 • Head of a Peasant Woman
with Red Cap, 1885**
Oil on canvas, 43 x 30 cm
Van Gogh Museum, Amsterdam

**107 • Head of a Peasant Woman
with Dark Cap, 1885**
Oil on canvas, 42 x 34 cm
Van Gogh Museum, Amsterdam

**108 • Peasant Woman
Standing Indoors, 1885**
Oil on canvas on panel, 41 x 26 cm
Narodni muzej, Belgrade

**109 • Peasant Woman Sweeping
the Floor, 1885**
Oil on canvas on panel, 41 x 27 cm
Rijksmuseum Kröller-Müller, Otterlo

**110 • Peasant Woman at
the Spinning Wheel, 1885**
Oil on canvas, 41 x 32.5 cm
Van Gogh Museum, Amsterdam

**111 • Peasant Woman Peeling
Potatoes, 1885**
Oil on canvas, 41 x 31.5 cm
*The Metropolitan Museum of Art,
New York*

**112 • Peasant Woman Peeling
Potatoes, 1885**
Oil on canvas on panel, 42 x 32 cm
Private Collection

97 98 99

100 101

102 103 104

105 106 107

108 109 110

111 112

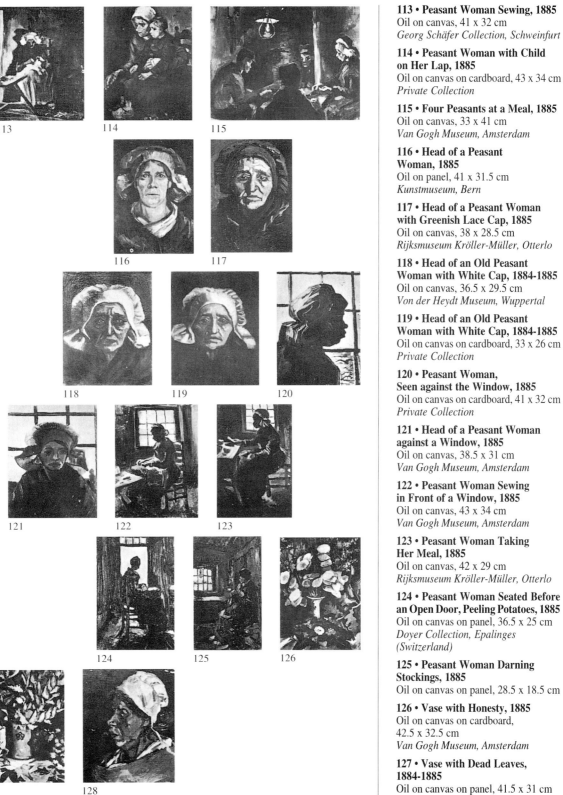

113

114

115

116

117

118

119

120

121

122

123

124

125

126

127

128

113 • Peasant Woman Sewing, 1885
Oil on canvas, 41 x 32 cm
Georg Schäfer Collection, Schweinfurt

**114 • Peasant Woman with Child
on Her Lap, 1885**
Oil on canvas on cardboard, 43 x 34 cm
Private Collection

115 • Four Peasants at a Meal, 1885
Oil on canvas, 33 x 41 cm
Van Gogh Museum, Amsterdam

**116 • Head of a Peasant
Woman, 1885**
Oil on panel, 41 x 31.5 cm
Kunstmuseum, Bern

**117 • Head of a Peasant Woman
with Greenish Lace Cap, 1885**
Oil on canvas, 38 x 28.5 cm
Rijksmuseum Kröller-Müller, Otterlo

**118 • Head of an Old Peasant
Woman with White Cap, 1884-1885**
Oil on canvas, 36.5 x 29.5 cm
Von der Heydt Museum, Wuppertal

**119 • Head of an Old Peasant
Woman with White Cap, 1884-1885**
Oil on canvas on cardboard, 33 x 26 cm
Private Collection

**120 • Peasant Woman,
Seen against the Window, 1885**
Oil on canvas on cardboard, 41 x 32 cm
Private Collection

**121 • Head of a Peasant Woman
against a Window, 1885**
Oil on canvas, 38.5 x 31 cm
Van Gogh Museum, Amsterdam

**122 • Peasant Woman Sewing
in Front of a Window, 1885**
Oil on canvas, 43 x 34 cm
Van Gogh Museum, Amsterdam

**123 • Peasant Woman Taking
Her Meal, 1885**
Oil on canvas, 42 x 29 cm
Rijksmuseum Kröller-Müller, Otterlo

**124 • Peasant Woman Seated Before
an Open Door, Peeling Potatoes, 1885**
Oil on canvas on panel, 36.5 x 25 cm
*Doyer Collection, Epalinges
(Switzerland)*

**125 • Peasant Woman Darning
Stockings, 1885**
Oil on canvas on panel, 28.5 x 18.5 cm

126 • Vase with Honesty, 1885
Oil on canvas on cardboard,
42.5 x 32.5 cm
Van Gogh Museum, Amsterdam

**127 • Vase with Dead Leaves,
1884-1885**
Oil on canvas on panel, 41.5 x 31 cm
Private Collection

128 • Head of a Peasant Woman, 1885
Oil on canvas, 41 x 35 cm
Private Collection

WORKS

129 • The Potato Eaters, 1885
Oil on canvas, 72 x 93 cm
Rijksmuseum Kröller-Müller, Otterlo

**130 • Peasant and Peasant
Woman Planting Potatoes, 1885**
Oil on canvas, 33 x 41 cm
Kunsthaus, Zurich

**131 • Water Mill at Opwetten,
1884-1885**
Oil on canvas on panel, 45 x 58 cm
Private Collection

132 • Landscape at Sunset, 1885
Oil on canvas, 27.5 x 41.5 cm
Private Collection

133 • Peasant Sitting at a Table, 1885
Oil on canvas, 44 x 32.5 cm
Rijksmuseum Kröller-Müller, Otterlo

**134 • Head of a Peasant with Cap,
1884-1885**
Oil on canvas, 39 x 30 cm
Private Collection

**135 • Still Life: Coffeepot
and White Bowls, 1885**
Oil on canvas, 23 x 35 cm
Private Collection

**136 • Head of a Peasant Woman
with White Cap, 1885**
Oil on canvas on panel, 45 x 36 cm
Van Gogh Museum, Amsterdam

**137 • Peasant Woman with
Winged Bonnet, 1885**
Oil on canvas on cardboard,
47.5 x 35.5 cm
*National Gallery of Scotland,
Edinburgh*

**138 • Head of a Peasant Woman
with White Cap, 1885**
Oil on canvas on panel, 41 x 32.5 cm
Private Collection

**139 • Head of a Peasant Woman
with White Cap, 1885**
Oil on canvas, 44 x 36 cm
Rijksmuseum Kröller-Müller, Otterlo

140 • Head of a Peasant Woman, 1885
Oil on canvas on panel, 47 x 34.5 cm
Private Collection

**141 • Head of a Peasant Woman
with White Cap, 1885**
Oil on canvas, 41 x 34.5 cm
Private Collection

**142 • Head of a Young Peasant
in a Peaked Cap, 1885**
Oil on canvas, 39 x 30.5 cm
*Musées royaux d'Art et d'Histoire,
Brussels*

143 • The Potato Eaters, 1885
Oil on canvas, 82 x 114 cm
Van Gogh Museum, Amsterdam

**144 • Head of a Young Peasant
with Pipe, 1884-1885**
Oil on canvas, 38 x 30 cm
Van Gogh Museum, Amsterdam

129

130

131

132

133

134

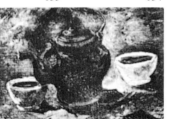

135

136

137

138

139

140

141

142

143

144

145

146

147

148

149

150

151

152

153

154

155

156

157

158

159

160

**145 • Head of a Peasant
with Hat, 1885**
Oil on canvas, 41.5 x 31.5 cm
Van Gogh Museum, Amsterdam

**146 • Head of a Peasant
Woman, 1885**
Oil on canvas, 40.5 x 34 cm
Rijksmuseum Kröller-Müller, Otterlo

**147 • Head of a Peasant Woman
with White Cap, 1885**
Oil on canvas, 43.5 x 35.5 cm
Van Gogh Museum, Amsterdam

**148 • Head of a Peasant Woman
in a Green Shawl, 1885**
Oil on canvas, 45.5 x 33 cm
Van Gogh Museum, Amsterdam

**149 • Head of a Peasant Woman
in a Green Shawl, 1885**
Oil on canvas, 45 x 35 cm
Musée des Beaux-Arts, Lyon

**150 • Still Life with Yellow
Straw Hat, 1885**
Oil on canvas, 36 x 53.5 cm
Rijksmuseum Kröller-Müller, Otterlo

**151 • Still Life with Earthenware
Pot, Bottle, and Clogs, 1885**
Oil on canvas on panel, 39 x 41.5 cm
Rijksmuseum Kröller-Müller, Otterlo

**152 • The Old Cemetery Tower
at Nuenen, 1885**
Oil on canvas, 63 x 79 cm
Van Gogh Museum, Amsterdam

153 • Cottage at Nightfall, 1885
Oil on canvas, 65.5 x 79 cm
Van Gogh Museum, Amsterdam

154 • Cottage, 1885
Oil on canvas, 35.5 x 67 cm
*John P. Natanson Collection,
Harrison (New York)*

**155 • Cottage and Woman
with Goat, 1885**
Oil on canvas, 60 x 85 cm
*Städelsches Kunstinstitut und
Städtische Galerie, Frankfurt*

156 • Cottage with Trees, 1885
Oil on canvas on panel, 32 x 46 cm
Private Collection

**157 • Cottage with Decrepit Barn
and Stooping Woman, 1885**
Oil on canvas, 62 x 113 cm
Private Collection

**158 • Cottage with Peasant Coming
Home, 1885**
Oil on canvas, 64 x 76 cm
Private Collection

**159 • Cottage with Woman
Digging, 1885**
Oil on canvas on cardboard,
31.3 x 42 cm
The Art Institute, Chicago

**160 • Cottage with Peasant
Woman Digging, 1885**
Oil on canvas on panel, 30.5 x 40 cm
Private Collection

WORKS

**161 • Peasant Woman
by the Fireplace, 1885**
Oil on canvas on panel, 29.5 x 40 cm
Private Collection

**162 • Peasant Woman by
the Fireplace, 1885**
Oil on canvas, 44 x 38 cm
*The Metropolitan Museum of Art,
New York*

**163 • Peasant Woman Sitting
on a Chair, 1885**
Oil on canvas, 34 x 26 cm

164 • Peasant Woman Digging, 1885
Oil on canvas on panel, 41.5 x 32 cm
Private Collection

165 • Peasant Woman Digging, 1885
Oil on canvas on panel, 37.5 x 25.7 cm
*Noordbrabants Museum,
Herzogenbusch*

166 • Peasant Woman Digging, 1885
Oil on canvas on panel, 42 x 32 cm
*Barber Institute of Fine Arts,
Birmingham*

167 • Peasant Woman Raking, 1885
Oil on canvas, 38.5 x 26.5 cm
Schweitzer Collection, New York

**168 • Peasant Woman
Laundering, 1885**
Oil on canvas, 29.5 x 36 cm
Private Collection

**169 • Peasant Woman Digging Up
Potatoes, 1885**
Oil on paper on panel, 31.5 x 38 cm
Musée royal des Beaux-Arts, Anvers

**170 • Peasant Woman Digging Up
Potatoes, 1885**
Oil on canvas on panel, 41 x 31 cm
Private Collection

**171 • Two Peasant Women Digging
Potatoes, 1885**
Oil on canvas on panel, 31.5 x 42.5 cm
Rijksmuseum Kröller-Müller, Otterlo

172 • Peasant Digging, 1885
Oil on canvas, 45.5 x 31.5 cm
Rijksmuseum Kröller-Müller, Otterlo

**173 • Sheaves of Wheat
in a Field, 1885**
Oil on canvas, 40 x 30 cm
Rijksmuseum Kröller-Müller, Otterlo

**174 • Still Life with a Basket of
Potatoes Surrounded by Autumn
Leaves and Vegetables, 1885**
Oil on canvas, 75 x 93 cm
Private Collection

**175 • Still Life with a Basket
of Vegetables, 1885**
Oil on canvas, 35.5 x 45 cm
*Anneliese Brand Collection,
Landsberg*

**176 • Still Life with Ginger Jar
and Onions, 1885**
Oil on canvas, 34 x 49.5 cm
Private Collection

161   162

163   164   165

166   167   168

169   170

171   172   173

174   175

176   177

178

179

180

181

182

183

184

185

186

187

188

189

190

191

192

177 • Still Life with Vegetables and Fruit, 1885
Oil on canvas, 32.5 x 43 cm
Van Gogh Museum, Amsterdam

178 • Still Life with Two Jars and Two Pumpkins, 1885
Oil on canvas on panel, 58 x 85 cm
Private Collection

179 • Still Life with a Basket of Apples and Two Pumpkins, 1885
Oil on canvas, 59 x 84.5 cm
Rijksmuseum Kröller-Müller, Otterlo

180 • Still Life with Ginger Jar and Apples, 1885
Oil on canvas on panel, 30.5 x 46.5 cm

181 • Still Life with an Earthen Bowl and Pears, 1885
Oil on canvas, 33 x 43.5 cm
Centraal Museum (on loan from the van Baaren Museum), Utrecht

182 • Still Life with a Basket of Apples, 1885
Oil on canvas, 30 x 47 cm

183 • Still Life with Basket of Apples, 1885
Oil on canvas, 33 x 43.5 cm
Van Gogh Museum, Amsterdam

184 • Still Life with Basket of Apples, 1885
Oil on canvas, 43 x 59 cm
Van Gogh Museum, Amsterdam

185 • Still Life with Copper Kettle, Jar, and Potatoes, 1885
Oil on canvas, 65.5 x 80.5 cm
Van Gogh Museum, Amsterdam

186 • Still Life with a Basket of Potatoes, 1885
Oil on canvas, 44.5 x 60 cm
Van Gogh Museum, Amsterdam

187 • Still Life with Two Baskets of Potatoes, 1885
Oil on canvas, 65.5 x 78.5 cm
Van Gogh Museum, Amsterdam

188 • Still Life with a Basket of Potatoes, 1885
Oil on canvas, 50.5 x 66 cm
Van Gogh Museum, Amsterdam

189 • Still Life with an Earthen Bowl and Potatoes, 1885
Oil on canvas, 44.5 x 57 cm
Brugmans-Beukema Collection, Gröningen

190 • Spinning Wheel, 1885
Oil on canvas, 34 x 44 cm
Van Gogh Museum, Amsterdam

191 • Still Life with Five Birds' Nests, 1885
Oil on canvas, 39.5 x 46 cm
Van Gogh Museum, Amsterdam

192 • Still Life with Three Birds' Nests, 1885
Oil on canvas on panel, 43 x 57 cm
Haags Gemeentemuseum, The Hague

WORKS

193 • Still Life with Three Birds' Nests, 1885
Oil on canvas, 33 x 42 cm
Rijksmuseum Kröller-Müller, Otterlo

194 • Still Life with Two Birds' Nests, 1885
Oil on canvas, 31.5 x 42.5 cm
Van Gogh Museum, Amsterdam

195 • Still Life with Three Birds' Nests, 1885
Oil on canvas, 33.5 x 50.5 cm
Rijksmusem Kröller-Müller, Otterlo

196 • The Green Parrot, 1885-1886
Oil on canvas on panel, 48 x 43 cm
Private Collection

197 • Ginger Jar Filled with Chrysanthemums, 1885-1886
Oil on canvas on panel, 40 x 29.5 cm
Private Collection

198 • View of Amsterdam, 1885
Oil on canvas on panel, 35 x 47 cm
Van Gogh Museum, Amsterdam

199 • View of Amsterdam from Central Station, 1885
Oil on panel, 19 x 25.5 cm
P. and N. de Boer Foundation, Amsterdam

200 • View of a Town with Drawbridge, 1885
Oil on panel, 42 x 49.5 cm
Van Meeteren-Van Diemen Arbeiter Collection, The Hague

201 • Still Life with Bible, 1885
Oil on canvas, 65 x 78 cm
Van Gogh Museum, Amsterdam

202 • Lane in Autumn, 1885
Oil on canvas on panel, 46 x 35 cm
Jäggli-Hahnloser Collection, Winterthur

203 • Country Lane with Two Figures, 1885
Oil on canvas on panel, 30 x 39.5 cm
Private Collection

204 • Landscape at Dusk, 1885
Oil on canvas on cardboard, 35 x 43 cm
Thyssen-Bornemisza Foundation, Lugano Castagnola

205 • Autumn Landscape, 1885
Oil on canvas on panel, 64.8 x 86.4 cm
Fitzwilliam Museum, Cambridge

206 • Autumn Landscape at Dusk, 1885
Oil on canvas on panel, 51 x 93 cm
Centraal Museum, Utrecht

207 • Avenue of Poplars at Sunset, 1885
Oil on canvas, 45.5 x 32.5 cm
Rijksmuseum Kröller-Müller, Otterlo

208 • The Willow, 1885
Oil on panel, 42 x 30 cm

193

194

195

196

197

198

199

200

201 202 203

204 205

206

207

208

209

210

211

212

213

214

215

216

217

218

219

220

221

222

223

224

209 • Autumn Landscape with Four Trees, 1885
Oil on canvas, 64 x 89 cm
Rijksmuseum Kröller-Müller, Otterlo

210 • The Vicarage at Nuenen, 1885
Oil on canvas, 33 x 43 cm
Van Gogh Museum, Amsterdam

211 • The Vicarage at Nuenen by Moonlight, 1885
Oil on canvas, 41 x 54.5 cm

212 • Backyards of Old Houses in Antwerp in the Snow, 1885
Oil on canvas, 44 x 33.5 cm
Van Gogh Museum, Amsterdam

213 • Quayside with Ships in Antwerp, 1885
Oil on panel, 20.5 x 27 cm
Van Gogh Museum, Amsterdam

214 • Portrait of an Old Man with Beard, 1885
Oil on canvas, 44 x 33.5 cm
Van Gogh Museum, Amsterdam

215 • Head of an Old Woman with White Cap (The Midwife), 1885
Oil on canvas, 50 x 40 cm
Van Gogh Museum, Amsterdam

216 • Head of a Woman with Her Hair Loose, 1885
Oil on canvas, 35 x 24 cm
Van Gogh Museum, Amsterdam

217 • Portrait of a Woman with Red Ribbon, 1885
Oil on canvas, 60 x 50 cm
Alfred Wyler Collection, New York

218 • Skull with Burning Cigarette, 1885-1886
Oil on canvas, 32 x 24.5 cm
Van Gogh Museum, Amsterdam

219 • Glass with Hellebores, 1885 (?)
Oil on canvas on panel, 31 x 22.5 cm

220 • Lane with Poplars, 1885-1886
Oil on canvas, 78 x 97.5 cm
Boymans-van Beuningen Museum, Rotterdam

221 • Still Life: Lemons, 1885-1886
Oil on canvas on panel, 34.5 x 50 cm
Hirschland Collection, Berkeley Heights (New Jersey)

222 • Self-Portrait with Dark Felt Hat at the Easel, 1886
Oil on canvas, 46.5 x 38.5 cm
Van Gogh Museum, Amsterdam

223 • Self-Portrait with Dark Felt Hat, 1886
Oil on canvas, 41.5 x 32.5 cm
Van Gogh Museum, Amsterdam

224 • Self-Portrait with Pipe, 1886
Oil on canvas, 27 x 19 cm
Van Gogh Museum, Amsterdam

WORKS

225 • Self-Portrait with Pipe, 1886
Oil on canvas, 46 x 38 cm
Van Gogh Museum, Amsterdam

**226 • Self-Portrait with Pipe
and Glass, 1886**
Oil on canvas, 61 x 50 cm
Van Gogh Museum, Amsterdam

227 • Self-Portrait, 1886
Oil on canvas, 39.5 x 29.5 cm
Haags Gemeentemuseum, The Hague

228 • Portrait of a Woman, 1886
Oil on canvas, 27 x 22 cm
Van Gogh Museum, Amsterdam

229 • Portrait of a Woman, 1886
Oil on canvas, 27 x 18.5 cm
Van Gogh Museum, Amsterdam

230 • Portrait of a Woman, 1886
Oil on canvas, 31.5 x 21.5 cm
Van Gogh Museum, Amsterdam

**231 • Nude of a Young Girl,
Seated, 1886**
Oil on canvas, 27 x 22.5 cm
Van Gogh Museum, Amsterdam

232 • The Kingfisher, 1886
Oil on canvas, 19 x 26.5 cm
Van Gogh Museum, Amsterdam

233 • Stuffed Kalong, 1886
Oil on canvas, 41 x 79 cm
Van Gogh Museum, Amsterdam

**234 • Still Life with Meat,
Vegetables, and Pottery, 1886**
Oil on canvas, 33.5 x 41 cm

235 • Still Life, 1886
Oil on canvas, 54 x 45 cm
Museu de Arte, São Paulo

**236 • Still Life with Apples,
Meat, and a Roll, 1886**
Oil on canvas, 46 x 55 cm
Rijksmuseum Kröller-Müller, Otterlo

237 • Tambourine with Pansies, 1886
Oil on canvas, 46 x 55.5 cm
Van Gogh Museum, Amsterdam

**238 • Lane at the Jardin
du Luxembourg, 1886**
Oil on canvas, 27.5 x 46 cm
*Sterling and Francine Clark Art
Institute, Williamstown
(Massachusetts)*

**239 • Sloping Path in
Montmartre, 1886**
Oil on cardboard, 22 x 16 cm
Van Gogh Museum, Amsterdam

240 • Le Moulin de la Galette, 1886
Oil on canvas, 38 x 46 cm
S. Brown Collection, Baden

225

226

227

228

229

230

231

232

233

234

235

236

237

238

239

240

241

242

243

244

245

246

247

248

249

250

251

252

253

254

255

256

241 • Le Moulin de la Galette, 1886
Oil on canvas, 38.5 x 46 cm
Rijksmuseum Kröller-Müller, Otterlo

242 • Le Moulin de la Galette, 1886
Oil on canvas, 38 x 46.5 cm
Nationalgalerie Staatliche Museen, Berlin

243 • Still Life with a Bottle, Two Glasses, Cheese, and Bread, 1886
Oil on canvas, 37.5 x 46 cm
Van Gogh Museum, Amsterdam

244 • Still Life, 1886
Oil on canvas, 32.5 x 46 cm
Scharenguival Collection

245 • Still Life : Mackerel, 1886
Oil on canvas, 39 x 56.5 cm
Oskar Reinhart Foundation, Winterthur

246 • Still Life : The Red Herrings, 1886
Oil on canvas, 21 x 42 cm
Rudolf Staechelin Foundation, Basel

247 • Still Life with Bloaters, 1886
Oil on canvas, 45 x 38 cm
Rijksmuseum Kröller-Müller, Otterlo

248 • The Bois de Boulogne with People Walking, 1886
Oil on canvas, 37.5 x 45.5 cm
Private Collection

249 • The Bois de Boulogne with People Walking, 1886
Oil on canvas, 37.5 x 45.5 cm
Hahnloser-Gassmann Collection, Zurich

250 • View of the Roofs of Paris, 1886
Oil on cardboard, 30 x 41 cm
Van Gogh Museum, Amsterdam

251 • The Pont du Carrousel and the Louvre, 1886
Oil on canvas, 31 x 44 cm
Private Collection

252 • Le Moulin de la Galette, 1886
Oil on canvas, 46 x 38 cm
Art Gallery and Museum, Glasgow

253 • Le Moulin de Blute-Fin, 1886
Oil on canvas, 46.5 x 38 cm
Bridgestone Museum, Tokyo

254 • The Fourteenth of July Celebration in Paris, 1886
Oil on canvas, 44 x 39 cm
Jäggli-Hahnloser Collection, Winterthur

255 • Twilight, before the Storm: Montmartre, 1886
Oil on cardboard, 14.8 x 10 cm
Private Collection

256 • Portrait of a Man, 1886-1887
Oil on canvas on panel, 31 x 39.5 cm
National Gallery of Victoria, Melbourne

WORKS

257 • Portrait of a Woman in Blue, 1885-1886
Oil on canvas, 46 x 38,5 cm
Van Gogh Museum, Amsterdam

258 • Vase with Carnations and Roses and a Bottle, 1886
Oil on canvas, 40 x 32 cm
Rijksmuseum Kröller-Müller, Otterlo

259 • Still Life with Scabiosa and Ranunculus, 1886
Oil on canvas, 26 x 20 cm
Private Collection

260 • Vase with Myosotis and Peonies, 1886
Oil on cardboard, 34.5 x 27.5 cm
Van Gogh Museum, Amsterdam

261 • Vase with Red and White Carnations on Yellow Background, 1886
Oil on canvas, 40 x 52 cm
Rijksmuseum Kröller-Müller, Otterlo

262 • Geranium in a Flowerpot, 1886
Oil on canvas, 46 x 38 cm
Private Collection

263 • Glass with Roses, 1886
Oil on cardboard, 35 x 27 cm
Van Gogh Museum, Amsterdam

264 • Vase with Carnations, 1886
Oil on canvas, 46 x 37.5 cm
Stedelijk Museum, Amsterdam

265 • Vase with Zinnias and Other Flowers, 1886
Oil on canvas, 50.2 x 61 cm
National Gallery of Canada, Ottawa

266 • Vase with Asters, Salvia, and Other Flowers, 1886
Oil on canvas, 70.5 x 34 cm
Haags Gemeentemuseum, The Hague

267 • Vase with Gladioli and Lilac, 1886
Oil on canvas, 69 x 33.5 cm
Eldwin McClellan Johnston Collection, Ballwin

268 • Still Life with Hollyhocks, 1886
Oil on canvas, 91 x 50.5 cm
Kunsthaus, Zurich

269 • Vase with Carnations and Other Flowers, 1886
Oil on canvas, 61 x 38 cm
David Loyd Kreeger Collection, Washington

270 • Vase with Carnations, 1886
Oil on canvas, 40 x 32.5 cm
Willem van der Vorm Foundation, Rotterdam

271 • White Vase with Roses and Other Flowers, 1886
Oil on canvas, 37 x 25.5 cm
Private Collection

272 • Still Life : Vase with Flowers, 1886
Oil on canvas, 65 x 54 cm
Museum of Modern Art, Cairo

257

258

259

260

261

262

263

264

265

266

267

268

269

270

271

272

273

274

275

276

277

278

279

280

281

282

283

284

285

286

287

288

273 • Vase with Asters and Phlox, 1886
Oil on canvas, 61 x 46 cm
Van Gogh Museum, Amsterdam

274 • Vase with Carnations, 1886
Oil on canvas, 46 x 38 cm
*Mrs. Murphy Collection,
New York*

275 • Vase with Zinnias and Geraniums, 1886
Oil on canvas, 61 x 45.9 cm
National Gallery of Canada, Ottawa

276 • Vase with Gladioli and Carnations, 1886
Oil on canvas, 78.5 x 40.5 cm
Private Collection

277 • Vase with Red Gladioli, 1886
Oil on canvas, 65 x 35 cm
Private Collection

278 • Vase with Gladioli and Carnations, 1886
Oil on canvas, 65.5 x 35 cm
*Boymans-van Beuningen Museum,
Rotterdam*

279 • Vase with Gladioli, 1886
Oil on canvas, 46.5 x 38,5 cm
Van Gogh Museum, Amsterdam

280 • Vase with Red Gladioli, 1886
Oil on canvas, 65 x 40 cm
Private Collection

281 • Coleus Plant in a Flowerpot, 1886
Oil on canvas, 42 x 22 cm
Van Gogh Museum, Amsterdam

282 • Montmartre Path with Sunflowers, 1886-1887
Oil on canvas, 35.5 x 27 cm
Museum of Modern Art, San Francisco

283 • View of Montmartre With Quarry, 1886
Oil on canvas, 22 x 33 cm
Van Gogh Museum, Amsterdam

284 • Montmartre: Quarry, the Mills, 1886
Oil on canvas, 32 x 41 cm
Van Gogh Museum, Amsterdam

285 • Montmartre: Quarry, the Mills, 1886
Oil on canvas, 56.2 x 62.5 cm
Van Gogh Museum, Amsterdam

286 • View of Montmartre with Windmills, 1886
Oil on canvas, 36 x 61 cm
Rijksmuseum Kröller-Müller, Otterlo

287 • View of the Roofs of Paris, 1886
Oil on canvas, 54 x 72.5 cm
Van Gogh Museum, Amsterdam

288 • View of Paris from Montmartre, 1886
Oil on canvas, 38.5 x 61.5 cm
Kunstmuseum, Basel

WORKS

289 • View of Paris from Vicinity of Montmartre, 1886
Oil on canvas, 44.5 x 37 cm
Private Collection

290 • Outskirts of Paris, 1886
Oil on canvas on cardboard,
45.7 x 54.6 cm
Private Collection

291 • "La Guinguette", Montmartre, 1886
Oil on canvas, 49 x 64 cm
Musée d'Orsay, Paris

292 • Vase with Red Poppies, 1886
Oil on canvas, 56 x 46.5 cm
Wadsworth Atheneum, Hartford

293 • Vase with Poppies, Cornflowers, Peonies, and Chrysanthemums, 1886
Oil on canvas, 99 x 79 cm
Rijksmuseum Kröller-Müller, Otterlo

294 • Vase with Daisies, 1886
Oil on paper on panel, 40 x 56 cm
The Museum of Art, Philadelphia

295 • Bowl with Peonies and Roses, 1886
Oil on canvas, 59 x 71 cm
Rijksmuseum Kröller-Müller, Otterlo

296 • Bowl with Sunflowers, Roses, and Other Flowers, 1886
Oil on canvas, 50 x 61 cm
Städtische Kunsthalle, Mannheim

297 • Cineraria in a Flowerpot, 1886
Oil on canvas, 54.5 x 46 cm
Museum Boymans-van Beuningen, Rotterdam

298 • Still Life with Mussels and Shrimps, 1886
Oil on canvas, 26.5 x 34.5 cm
Van Gogh Museum, Amsterdam

299 • Man's Portrait, 1886
Oil on canvas, 55 x 41 cm

300 • A Pair of Shoes, 1886
Oil on canvas, 37.5 x 45.5 cm
Van Gogh Museum, Amsterdam

301 • Imperial Crown Fritillaries in a Copper Vase, 1886
Oil on canvas, 73 x 60.5 cm
Musée d'Orsay, Paris

302 • Three Pairs of Shoes, 1886-1887
Oil on canvas, 49 x 72 cm
The Fogg Art Museum, Cambridge (Massachusetts)

303 • A Pair of Shoes, 1886-1887
Oil on canvas, 37.5 x 45.5 cm
Emil Schumacher Collection, Brussels

304 • Plaster Statuette of a Female Torso, 1886-1887
Oil on canvas, 73 x 54 cm
Private Collection

305 • Plaster Statuette of a Female Torso, 1886-1887
Oil on cardboard, 46 x 38 cm
Van Gogh Museum, Amsterdam

289

290

291

292

293

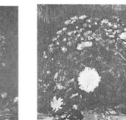
294

295

296

297

298

299

300

301

302

303

304

305 306 307

308 309

310 311 312

313 314 315

316 317 318

319 320

306 • Plaster Statuette of a Female Torso, 1886-1887
Oil on canvas, 40.5 x 27 cm
Van Gogh Museum, Amsterdam

307 • Plaster Statuette of a Female Torso, 1886-1887
Oil on cardboard, 46.5 x 38 cm
Van Gogh Museum, Amsterdam

308 • Plaster Statuette of a Female Torso, 1886-1887
Oil on canvas, 41 x 32.5 cm
Van Gogh Museum, Amsterdam

309 • Plaster Statuette of a Female Torso, 1886-1887
Oil on cardboard, 35 x 27 cm
Van Gogh Museum, Amsterdam

310 • Plaster Statuette of a Female Torso, 1886-1887
Oil on cardboard, 35 x 27 cm
Van Gogh Museum, Amsterdam

311 • Plaster Statuette of a Female Torso, 1886-1887
Oil on cardboard, 32.5 x 24 cm
Van Gogh Museum, Amsterdam

312 • Plaster Statuette of a Male Torso, 1886-1887
Oil on cardboard, 35 x 27 cm
Van Gogh Museum, Amsterdam

313 • Plaster Statuette of a Kneeling Man, 1886-1887
Oil on cardboard, 35 x 27 cm
Van Gogh Museum, Amsterdam

314 • Plaster Statuette of a Horse, 1886-1887
Oil on cardboard, 33 x 41 cm
Van Gogh Museum, Amsterdam

315 • Le Moulin de la Galette, 1886-1887
Oil on canvas, 55 x 38.5 cm
W. Engelhard Collection, Newark

316 • Le Moulin de la Galette, 1886-1887
Oil on canvas, 61 x 50 cm
Museo Nacional de las Bellas Artes, Buenos Aires

317 • Montmartre Near the Upper Mill, 1886-1887
Oil on canvas, 44 x 33.5 cm
The Art Institute, Chicago

318 • Old Tanguy (Père Tanguy), 1886-1887
Oil on canvas, 47 x 38.5 cm
Ny Carlsberg Glyptotek, Copenhagen

319 • The Art Dealer Alexander Reid, 1887
Oil on cardboard, 41 x 33 cm
Mrs. Weitzenhoffer Collection, Oklahoma City

320 • Agostina Segatori Sitting in the Café du Tambourin, 1887
Oil on canvas, 55.5 x 46.5 cm
Van Gogh Museum, Amsterdam

WORKS

321 • Vase with Flowers, Coffeepot, and Fruit, 1887
Oil on canvas, 41 x 38 cm
Von der Heydt Museum, Wuppertal

322 • A Plate of Rolls, 1887
Oil on canvas, 31.5 x 40 cm
Van Gogh Museum, Amsterdam

323 • Still Life with Lemons on a Plate, 1887
Oil on canvas, 21 x 26.5 cm
Van Gogh Museum, Amsterdam

324 • Still Life with Decanter and Lemons on a Plate, 1887
Oil on canvas, 46.5 x 38.5 cm
Van Gogh Museum, Amsterdam

325 • Still Life with a Basket of Crocuses, 1887
Oil on canvas, 32.5 x 41 cm
Van Gogh Museum, Amsterdam

326 • Basket of Sprouting Bulbs, 1887
Oil on canvas, 31.5 x 48 cm
Van Gogh Museum, Amsterdam

327 • Still Life with Three Books, 1887
Oil on panel, 31 x 48.5 cm
Van Gogh Museum, Amsterdam

328 • Still Life with Absinthe, 1887
Oil on canvas, 46.5 x 33 cm
Van Gogh Museum, Amsterdam

329 • Factories Seen from a Hillside in Moonlight, 1887
Oil on canvas, 21 x 46.5 cm
Van Gogh Museum, Amsterdam

330 • Boulevard de Clichy, 1887
Oil on canvas, 45.5 x 55 cm
Van Gogh Museum, Amsterdam

331 • View of Paris from Vincent's Room in the Rue Lepic, 1887
Oil on canvas, 46 x 38 cm
Van Gogh Museum, Amsterdam

332 • View of Paris from Vincent's Room in the Rue Lepic, 1887
Oil on canvas, 46 x 38 cm
Private Collection

333 • Le Moulin de la Galette, 1887
Oil on canvas, 46 x 38 cm
Carnegie Institute, Museum of Art, Pittsburgh

334 • Vegetable Gardens in Montmartre, 1887
Oil on canvas, 44.8 x 81 cm
Van Gogh Museum, Amsterdam

335 • Street Scene in Montmartre: Le Moulin à Poivre, 1887
Oil on canvas, 34.5 x 64.5 cm
Van Gogh Museum, Amsterdam

321

322

323

324

325

326

327

328

329

330

331

332

333

334

335

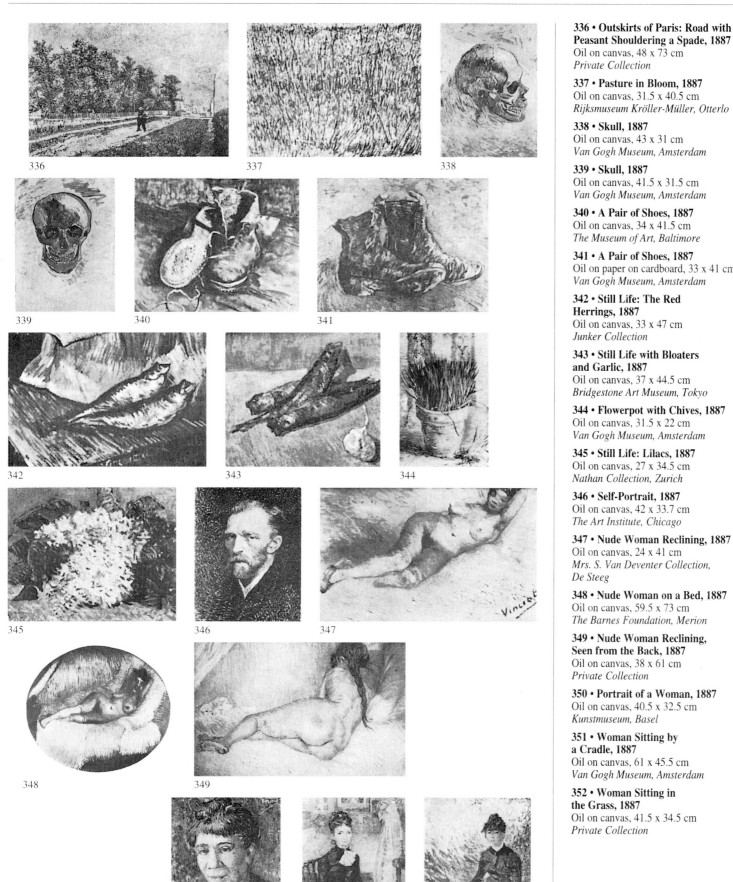

336

337

338

339

340

341

342

343

344

345

346

347

348

349

350

351

352

336 • Outskirts of Paris: Road with Peasant Shouldering a Spade, 1887
Oil on canvas, 48 x 73 cm
Private Collection

337 • Pasture in Bloom, 1887
Oil on canvas, 31.5 x 40.5 cm
Rijksmuseum Kröller-Müller, Otterlo

338 • Skull, 1887
Oil on canvas, 43 x 31 cm
Van Gogh Museum, Amsterdam

339 • Skull, 1887
Oil on canvas, 41.5 x 31.5 cm
Van Gogh Museum, Amsterdam

340 • A Pair of Shoes, 1887
Oil on canvas, 34 x 41.5 cm
The Museum of Art, Baltimore

341 • A Pair of Shoes, 1887
Oil on paper on cardboard, 33 x 41 cm
Van Gogh Museum, Amsterdam

342 • Still Life: The Red Herrings, 1887
Oil on canvas, 33 x 47 cm
Junker Collection

343 • Still Life with Bloaters and Garlic, 1887
Oil on canvas, 37 x 44.5 cm
Bridgestone Art Museum, Tokyo

344 • Flowerpot with Chives, 1887
Oil on canvas, 31.5 x 22 cm
Van Gogh Museum, Amsterdam

345 • Still Life: Lilacs, 1887
Oil on canvas, 27 x 34.5 cm
Nathan Collection, Zurich

346 • Self-Portrait, 1887
Oil on canvas, 42 x 33.7 cm
The Art Institute, Chicago

347 • Nude Woman Reclining, 1887
Oil on canvas, 24 x 41 cm
Mrs. S. Van Deventer Collection, De Steeg

348 • Nude Woman on a Bed, 1887
Oil on canvas, 59.5 x 73 cm
The Barnes Foundation, Merion

349 • Nude Woman Reclining, Seen from the Back, 1887
Oil on canvas, 38 x 61 cm
Private Collection

350 • Portrait of a Woman, 1887
Oil on canvas, 40.5 x 32.5 cm
Kunstmuseum, Basel

351 • Woman Sitting by a Cradle, 1887
Oil on canvas, 61 x 45.5 cm
Van Gogh Museum, Amsterdam

352 • Woman Sitting in the Grass, 1887
Oil on canvas, 41.5 x 34.5 cm
Private Collection

WORKS

**353 • A Woman Walking
in a Garden, 1887**
Oil on canvas, 48 x 60 cm
Private Collection

354 • Park at Asnières in Spring, 1887
Oil on canvas, 50 x 65 cm
Singer Museum, Laren

355 • Chestnut Tree in Bloom, 1887
Oil on canvas, 56 x 46.5 cm
Van Gogh Museum, Amsterdam

356 • On the Outskirts of Paris, 1887
Oil on canvas, 38 x 46 cm
Private Collection

357 • The Banks of the Seine, 1887
Oil on canvas, 32 x 46 cm
Van Gogh Museum, Amsterdam

358 • The Seine with a Rowboat, 1887
Oil on canvas, 55 x 65 cm
Private Collection

**359 • Fishing in the Spring,
Pont de Clichy, 1887**
Oil on canvas, 49 x 58 cm
The Art Institute, Chicago

**360 • The Banks of the Seine
with Boats, 1887**
Oil on canvas, 48 x 55 cm
Private Collection

**361 • View of a River with
Rowboats, 1887**
Oil on canvas, 52 x 65 cm
*William Middleton Collection,
Aberdeen*

**362 • Roadway with Underpass
(The Viaduct), 1887**
Oil on canvas, 31.5 x 40.5 cm
*The Solomon R. Guggenheim Museum,
New York*

**363 • Bridges Across the Seine
at Asnières, 1887**
Oil on canvas, 52 x 65 cm
Bührle Collection, Zurich

**364 • The Seine Bridge
at Asnières, 1887**
Oil on canvas, 53 x 73 cm
Menil Collection, Houston

**365 • Walk Along the Banks
of the Seine Near Asnières, 1887**
Oil on canvas, 49 x 65.5 cm
Van Gogh Museum, Amsterdam

**366 • Entrance of the Voyer
d'Argenson Park at Asnières, 1887**
Oil on canvas, 55 x 67 cm
Private Collection

**367 • Couples in the Voyer
d'Argenson Park at Asnières, 1887**
Oil on canvas, 75 x 112.5 cm
Van Gogh Museum, Amsterdam

**368 • Lane in Voyer d'Argenson
Park at Asnières, 1887**
Oil on canvas on cardboard, 33 x 42 cm
Van Gogh Museum, Amsterdam

353

354

355

356

357

358

359

360

361

362

363

364

365

366

367

368

369

371

372

373

374

375

376

377

378

379

380

381

382

383

384

369 • Lane in Voyer d'Argenson Park at Asnières, 1887
Oil on canvas, 59 x 81 cm
Yale University Art Gallery, New Haven

370 • Avenue in Voyer d'Argenson Park at Asnières, 1887
Oil on canvas, 55 x 67 cm
Mrs. Gilman Collection, New York

371 • Corner of Voyer d'Argenson Park at Asnières, 1887
Oil on canvas, 49 x 65 cm
Private Collection

372 • Le Restaurant Rispal, 1887
Oil on canvas, 72 x 60 cm
Henry W. Block, Shanwee Mission (Kansas)

373 • The Restaurant de la Sirène at Asnières, 1887
Oil on canvas, 51.5 x 64 cm
Ashmolean Museum, Oxford

374 • Restaurant de la Sirène at Asnières, 1887
Oil on canvas, 54.5 x 65.5 cm
Musée d'Orsay, Paris

375 • Bathing Float on the Seine at Asnières, 1887
Oil on canvas, 19 x 27 cm
Virginia Museum of Fine Arts, Richmond

376 • The Factory at Asnières, 1887
Oil on canvas, 46.5 x 54 cm
The Barnes Foundation, Merion

377 • Factories at Asnières Seen from the Quai de Clichy, 1887
Oil on canvas, 54 x 72 cm
The Art Museum, Saint Louis

378 • Exterior of a Restaurant at Asnières, 1887
Oil on canvas, 18.5 x 27 cm
Van Gogh Museum, Amsterdam

379 • Japonaiserie: Flowering Plum Tree, 1887
Oil on canvas, 55 x 46 cm
Van Gogh Museum, Amsterdam

380 • Japonaiserie: Bridge in the Rain, 1887
Oil on canvas, 73 x 54 cm
Van Gogh Museum, Amsterdam

381 • Japonaiserie: Oiran, 1887
Oil on canvas, 105.5 x 60.5 cm
Van Gogh Museum, Amsterdam

382 • Vegetable Gardens at Montmartre, 1887
Oil on canvas, 81 x 100 cm
Van Gogh Museum, Amsterdam

383 • Vegetable Gardens in Montmartre: La Butte Montmartre, 1887
Oil on canvas, 96 x 120 cm
Stedelijk Museum, Amsterdam

384 • Trees in a Field on a Sunny Day, 1887
Oil on canvas, 37.5 x 46 cm
P. and N. de Boer Foundation, Amsterdam

WORKS

385 • Wheat Field with a Lark, 1887
Oil on canvas, 54 x 65.5 cm
Van Gogh Museum, Amsterdam

**386 • Edge of a Wheat Field
with Poppies, 1887**
Oil on canvas on cardboard,
40 x 32.5 cm
Private Collection

387 • Path in the Woods, 1887
Oil on canvas, 46 x 38.5 cm
Van Gogh Museum, Amsterdam

388 • Trees and Undergrowth, 1887
Oil on canvas, 46.5 x 55.5 cm
Van Gogh Museum, Amsterdam

389 • Trees and Undergrowth, 1887
Oil on canvas, 46.5 x 36 cm
Van Gogh Museum, Amsterdam

390 • Undergrowth, 1887
Oil on canvas, 46 x 38 cm
*Cantraal Museum (on loan from the
van Baaren Museum), Utrecht*

391 • Undergrowth, 1887
Oil on canvas, 46 x 38 cm
Van Gogh Museum, Amsterdam

**392 • Vase with Cornflowers
and Poppies, 1887**
Oil on canvas, 80 x 67 cm

**393 • Vase with Lilacs, Daisies,
and Anemones, 1887**
Oil on canvas, 46.5 x 37.5 cm
Private Collection

394 • Flowers in a Vase, 1887
Oil on canvas, 61 x 38 cm
Rijksmuseum Kröller-Müller, Otterlo

**395 • Banks of the Seine with Pont
de Clichy in the Spring, 1887**
Oil on canvas, 50 x 60 cm
Museum of Art, Dallas

**396 • Banks of the Seine with
the Pont de Clichy, 1887**
Oil on cardboard, 30.5 x 39 cm
Niarchos Collection, Athens

**397 • The Seine with the Pont
de Clichy, 1887**
Oil on canvas, 54 x 46 cm
Private Collection

**398 • The Seine with the Pont
de la Grande Jatte, 1887**
Oil on canvas, 32 x 40.5 cm
Van Gogh Museum, Amsterdam

399 • Interior of a Restaurant, 1887
Oil on canvas, 45.5 x 56.5 cm
Rijksmuseum Kröller-Müller, Otterlo

400 • Garden with Sunflower, 1887
Oil on canvas, 42.5 x 35.5 cm
Van Gogh Museum, Amsterdam

385

386

387

388

389

390

391

392

393

394

395

396

397

398

399

400

401

402

403

404

405

406

407

408

409

410

411

412

413

414

415

416

401 • Portrait of Art Dealer Alexander Reid, 1887
Oil on cardboard, 41.5 x 33.5 cm
Art Gallery and Museum, Glasgow

402 • Self-Portrait, 1887
Oil on cardboard, 19 x 14 cm
Van Gogh Museum, Amsterdam

403 • Self-Portrait, 1887
Oil on canvas, 41 x 33 cm
Van Gogh Museum, Amsterdam

404 • Self-Portrait, 1887
Oil on canvas on cardboard,
42.5 x 31.5 cm
Van Gogh Museum, Amsterdam

405 • Self-Portrait with Straw Hat and Pipe, 1887
Oil on canvas, 41.5 x 31.5 cm
Van Gogh Museum, Amsterdam

406 • Self-Portrait, 1887
Oil on cardboard, 19 x 14 cm
Van Gogh Museum, Amsterdam

407 • Self-Portrait, 1887
Oil on canvas on cardboard, 41 x 31 cm
Van Gogh Museum, Amsterdam

408 • Self-Portrait, 1887
Oil on canvas, 41 x 33.5 cm
Wadsworth Atheneum, Hartford

409 • Self-Portrait, 1887
Oil on canvas, 42 x 34 cm
Van Gogh Museum, Amsterdam

410 • Self-Portrait with Straw Hat, 1887
Oil on canvas, 40.5 x 32.5 cm
Van Gogh Museum, Amsterdam

411 • Self-Portrait, 1887
Oil on cardboard, 19 x 14 cm
Van Gogh Museum, Amsterdam

412 • Self-Portrait, 1887
Oil on cardboard, 41 x 32 cm
Stedelijk Museum, Amsterdam

413 • Self-Portrait with Straw Hat, 1887
Oil on canvas on panel, 35.5 x 27 cm
The Institute of Arts, Detroit

414 • Self-Portrait, 1887
Oil on canvas, 41 x 33 cm
Van Gogh Museum, Amsterdam

415 • Self-Portrait, 1887
Oil on paper, 34.2 x 25.5 cm
Rijksmuseum Kröller-Müller, Otterlo

416 • Self-Portrait with Gray Felt Hat, 1887
Oil on canvas, 44 x 37.5 cm
Van Gogh Museum, Amsterdam

WORKS

417 • Two Cut Sunflowers, 1887
Oil on canvas, 21 x 27 cm
Van Gogh Museum, Amsterdam

**418 • Sunflowers
(Two Cut Sunflowers), 1887**
Oil on canvas, 43.2 x 61 cm
*The Metropolitan Museum of Art,
New York*

419 • Two Cut Sunflowers, 1887
Oil on canvas, 50 x 60 cm
Kunstmuseum, Bern

420 • Four Cut Sunflowers, 1887
Oil on canvas, 60 x 100 cm
Rijksmuseum Kröller-Müller, Otterlo

**421 • Still Life with Plaster
Statuette, a Rose,
and Two Novels, 1887**
Oil on canvas, 55 x 46.5 cm
Rijksmuseum Kröller-Müller, Otterlo

422 • Still Life: French Novels, 1887
Oil on canvas, 53 x 73.5 cm
Van Gogh Museum, Amsterdam

**423 • Still Life with French Novels
and a Rose, 1887**
Oil on canvas, 73 x 93 cm
Private Collection

**424 • Still Life with Red Cabbages
and Onions, 1887**
Oil on canvas, 50 x 64.5 cm
Van Gogh Museum, Amsterdam

425 • Still Life with Grapes, 1887
Oil on canvas, 32.5 x 46 cm
Van Gogh Museum, Amsterdam

**426 • Still Life with Grapes, Pears,
and Lemons, 1887**
Oil on canvas, 48.5 x 65 cm
Van Gogh Museum, Amsterdam

**427 • Still Life with Grapes, Apples,
Pears, and Lemons, 1887**
Oil on canvas, 44 x 58.7 cm
The Art Institute, Chicago

428 • Still Life with Apples, 1887
Oil on canvas, 45.5 x 61 cm
Van Gogh Museum, Amsterdam

**429 • Still Life with Basket
of Apples, 1887**
Oil on canvas, 50 x 61 cm
Rijksmuseum Kröller-Müller, Otterlo

**430 • Still Life with Basket
of Apples, 1887**
Oil on canvas, 46.7 x 55.2 cm
Schoenberg Collection, Saint Louis

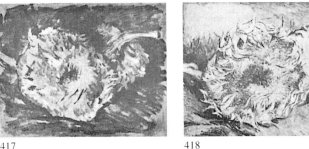

417

418

419

420

421

422

423

424

425

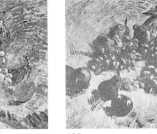

426

427

428

429

430

431 432 433

434 435 436

437 438 439

440 441 442

4433  444 445

 447

446 447 448

431 • Self-Portrait, 1887
Oil on canvas, 46.5 x 35.5 cm
Bührle Collection, Zurich

432 • Self-Portrait, 1887
Oil on canvas, 46 x 38 cm
Kunsthistorisches Museum, Vienna

433 • Self-Portrait, 1887
Oil on canvas, 44.1 x 35.1 cm
Musée d'Orsay, Paris

**434 • Portrait of a Man
with a Skull Cap, 1887**
Oil on canvas, 65.5 x 54.5 cm
Van Gogh Museum, Amsterdam

435 • Old Tanguy (Père Tanguy), 1887
Oil on canvas, 92 x 73 cm
Musée Rodin, Paris

436 • Old Tanguy (Père Tanguy), 1887
Oil on canvas, 65 x 51 cm
Niarchos Collection, Athens

**437 • Self-Portrait with
a Japanese Print, 1887**
Oil on canvas, 44 x 35 cm
Kunstmuseum, Basel

**438 • The Italian Woman
(Agostina Segatori), 1887**
Oil on canvas, 81 x 60 cm
Musée d'Orsay, Paris

**439 • Self-Portrait with
Straw Hat, 1887**
Oil on canvas, 40.6 x 31.8 cm
*The Metropolitan Museum of Art,
New York*

440 • Self-Portrait at the Easel, 1888
Oil on canvas, 65.5 x 50.5 cm
Van Gogh Museum, Amsterdam

441 • Landscape with Snow, 1888
Oil on canvas, 38 x 46 cm
*The Solomon R. Guggenheim Museum,
New York*

442 • An Old Woman of Arles, 1888
Oil on canvas, 58 x 42.5 cm
Van Gogh Museum, Amsterdam

443 • A Pork-Butcher's Shop, 1888
Oil on canvas on cardboard,
39.5 x 32.5 cm
Van Gogh Museum, Amsterdam

**444 • Snowy Landscape with Arles
in the Background, 1888**
Oil on canvas, 50 x 60 cm
Private Collection

**445 • The Gleize Bridge Over
the Vigueyret Canal, 1888**
Oil on canvas, 46 x 49 cm
Private Collection

**446 • Avenue of Plane Trees Near
Arles Station, 1888**
Oil on canvas, 46 x 49.5 cm
Musée Rodin, Paris

447 • Potatoes in a Yellow Dish, 1888
Oil on canvas, 39 x 47 cm
Rijksmuseum Kröller-Müller, Otterlo

448 • Basket with Six Oranges, 1888
Oil on canvas, 45 x 54 cm
Goulandris Collection, Lausanne

WORKS

449 • Blooming Almond Branch in a Glass, 1888
Oil on canvas, 24 x 19 cm
Van Gogh Museum, Amsterdam

450 • Still Life Blooming Almond Branch in a Glass with a Book, 1888
Oil on canvas, 24 x 19 cm
Private Collection

451 • Pink Peach Tree in Bloom, 1888
Oil on canvas, 73 x 59.5 cm
Rijksmuseum Kröller-Müller, Otterlo

452 • Apricot Trees in Bloom, 1888
Oil on canvas, 55 x 56.5 cm
Private Collection

453 • Orchard in Bloom, 1888
Oil on canvas, 55 x 65 cm
National Gallery of Scotland, Edinburgh

454 • Blooming Pear Tree, 1888
Oil on canvas, 73 x 46 cm
Van Gogh Museum, Amsterdam

455 • Orchard with Blooming Apricot Trees, 1888
Oil on canvas, 64.5 x 80.5 cm
Van Gogh Museum, Amsterdam

456 • Peach Tree in Bloom, 1888
Oil on canvas, 80.5 x 59.5 cm
Van Gogh Museum, Amsterdam

457 • The White Orchard, 1888
Oil on canvas, 60 x 81 cm
Van Gogh Museum, Amsterdam

458 • Orchard in Bloom, Bordered by Cypresses, 1888
Oil on canvas, 32.5 x 40 cm
Richard J. Bernhard Collection, New York

459 • Apricot Trees in Bloom, Near Arles, 1888
Oil on canvas, 41 x 33 cm
Continental Art Holdings Ltd. Collection, Johannesburg

460 • Orchard in Bloom, Bordered by Cypresses, 1888
Oil on canvas, 65 x 81 cm
Rijksmuseum Kröller-Müller, Otterlo

461 • Almond Tree in Bloom, 1888
Oil on canvas, 48.5 x 36 cm
Van Gogh Museum, Amsterdam

462 • Orchard with Peach Trees in Bloom, 1888
Oil on canvas, 65 x 81 cm
Private Collection

463 • Orchard in Bloom, 1888
Oil on canvas, 72 x 58 cm
Private Collection

464 • Orchard in Bloom, 1888
Oil on canvas, 72.4 x 53.5 cm
The Metropolitan Museum of Art, New York

449

450

451

452

453

454

455

456

457

458

459

460

461

462

463

464

465

466

467

468

469

470

471

472

473

474

475

476

477

478

479

480

465 • Orchard in Bloom, 1888
Oil on canvas, 72.5 x 92 cm
Van Gogh Museum, Amsterdam

**466 • The Langlois Bridge at Arles
with Women Washing, 1888**
Oil on canvas, 54 x 65 cm
Rijksmuseum Kröller-Müller, Otterlo

467 • Two Lovers, 1888
Oil on canvas, 32.5 x 23 cm
Private Collection

**468 • The Langlois Bridge
at Arles with Road Alongside
the Canal, 1888**
Oil on canvas, 59.5 x 74 cm
Van Gogh Museum, Amsterdam

**469 • The Langlois Bridge
at Arles, 1888**
Oil on canvas, 60 x 65 cm
Private Collection

**470 • The Langlois Bridge
at Arles, 1888**
Oil on canvas, 49.5 x 64 cm
Wallraf-Richartz Museum, Cologne

**471 • Landscape Under
a Stormy Sky, 1888**
Oil on canvas, 60 x 73 cm
Socindec Foundation, Vaduz

**472 • Path Through a Field
with Willows, 1888**
Oil on canvas, 31 x 38.5 cm

473 • Rose in Bloom, 1888
Oil on canvas, 33 x 42 cm
*National Museum of Western Art,
Tokyo*

**474 • View of Arles with Irises
in the Foreground, 1888**
Oil on canvas, 54 x 65 cm
Van Gogh Museum, Amsterdam

**475 • Farmhouse in
a Wheat Field, 1888**
Oil on canvas, 45 x 50 cm
Van Gogh Museum, Amsterdam

**476 • Still Life: Bottle, Lemons,
and Oranges, 1888**
Oil on canvas, 53 x 63 cm
Rijksmuseum Kröller-Müller, Otterlo

**477 • Still Life: Blue Enamel
Coffeepot, Earthenware,
and Fruit, 1888**
Oil on canvas, 65 x 81 cm
Goulandris Collection, Lausanne

**478 • Still Life: Majolica Jug
with Wildflowers, 1888**
Oil on canvas, 55 x 46 cm
The Barnes Foundation , Merion

479 • The Zouave, 1888
Oil on canvas, 65 x 54 cm
Van Gogh Museum, Amsterdam

480 • The Seated Zouave, 1888
Oil on canvas, 81 x 65 cm
Private Collection

116

WORKS

481 • Girl with Ruffled Hair, 1888
Oil on canvas, 35.5 x 24.5 cm
Private Collection

482 • Seascape at Saintes-Maries, 1888
Oil on canvas, 51 x 64 cm
Van Gogh Museum, Amsterdam

483 • Seascape at Saintes-Maries, 1888
Oil on canvas, 44 x 53 cm
Pushkin Museum, Moscow

**484 • Fishing Boats on the Beach
at Saintes-Maries, 1888**
Oil on canvas, 65 x 81.5 cm
Van Gogh Museum, Amsterdam

**485 • Three White Cottages
in Saintes-Maries, 1888**
Oil on canvas, 33.5 x 41.5 cm
Kunsthaus (on loan), Zurich

486 • Lane in Saintes-Maries, 1888
Oil on canvas, 38.3 x 46.1 cm
Private Collection

487 • View of Saintes-Maries, 1888
Oil on canvas, 64 x 53 cm
Rijksmuseum Kröller-Müller, Otterlo

488 • Farmhouse in Provence, 1888
Oil on canvas, 46 x 61 cm
National Gallery of Art, Washington

**489 • Haystacks Under a Rainy Sky,
1888-1890 (?)**
Oil on canvas, 64 x 52.5 cm
Rijksmuseum Kröller-Müller, Otterlo

490 • A Lane Near Arles, 1888
Oil on canvas, 61 x 50 cm
Kunstsammlungen, Coburg

**491 • The Bridge
at Trinquetaille, 1888**
Oil on canvas, 65 x 81 cm
Private Collection

**492 • The Roubine du roi Canal
with Washerwomen, 1888**
Oil on canvas, 74 x 60 cm
Private Collection

493 • Rocks with Oak Tree, 1888
Oil on canvas, 54 x 65 cm
The Museum of Fine Arts, Houston

**494 • Sunset: Wheat Fields
Near Arles, 1888**
Oil on canvas, 74 x 91 cm
Kunstmuseum, Winterthur

495 • The Sower, 1888
Oil on canvas, 64 x 80.5 cm
Rijksmuseum Kröller-Müller, Otterlo

496 • Wheat Field, 1888
Oil on canvas, 50 x 61.5 cm
*P. and N. de Boer Foundation,
Amsterdam*

481

482

483

484

485

486

487

488

489

490

491

492

493

494

495   496

497

498

499

500

501

502

503

504

505

506

507

508

509

510

511

512

497 • Wheat Field with the Alpilles Foothills in the Background, 1888
Oil on canvas on cardboard, 54 x 65 cm
Van Gogh Museum, Amsterdam

498 • Harvest at La Crau, with Montmajour in the Background, 1888
Oil on canvas, 73 x 92 cm
Van Gogh Museum, Amsterdam

499 • Harvest in Provence, 1888
Oil on canvas, 50 x 60 cm
Israel Museum, Jerusalem

500 • Haystacks in Provence, 1888
Oil on canvas, 73 x 92.5 cm
Rijksmuseum Kröller-Müller, Otterlo

501 • Green Ears of Wheat, 1888
Oil on canvas, 54 x 65 cm
Israel Museum, Jerusalem

502 • Wheatstacks with Reaper, 1888
Oil on canvas, 73 x 93 cm
Museum of Art, Toledo (Ohio)

503 • Wheatstacks with Reaper, 1888
Oil on canvas, 53 x 66 cm
Nationalmuseum, Stockholm

504 • Wheat Field with Sheaves, 1888
Oil on canvas, 55.2 x 66.6 cm
Academy of Arts, Honolulu

505 • Sunny Lawn in a Public Parks, 1888
Oil on canvas, 60.5 x 73.5 cm
Kunsthaus, Zurich

506 • Flowering Garden with Path, 1888
Oil on canvas, 72 x 91 cm
Haags Gemeentemuseum (on loan), The Hague

507 • Flowering Garden, 1888
Oil on canvas, 92 x 73 cm
The Metropolitan Museum of Art (on loan), New York

508 • La Mousmé, 1888
Oil on canvas, 74 x 60 cm
National Gallery of Art, Washington

509 • The Little Arlésienne, 1888
Oil on canvas, 51 x 49 cm
Rijksmuseum Kröller-Müller, Otterlo

510 • The Smoker, 1888
Oil on canvas, 62 x 47 cm
The Barnes Foundation, Merion

511 • Self-Portrait with Pipe and Straw Hat, 1888
Oil on canvas on cardboard, 42 x 30 cm
Van Gogh Museum, Amsterdam

512 • Interior of a Restaurant in Arles, 1888
Oil on canvas, 65.5 x 81 cm
Private Collection

WORKS

513 • Interior of the Restaurant Carrel in Arles, 1888
Oil on canvas, 54 x 64.5 cm
Danforth Collection, Providence

514 • Garden Behind a House, 1888
Oil on canvas, 63.5 x 52.5 cm
Kunsthaus (on loan), Zurich

515 • The Postman Roulin, 1888
Oil on canvas, 81.2 x 65.3 cm
Museum of Fine Arts, Boston

516 • The Postman Joseph Roulin, 1888
Oil on canvas, 64 x 48 cm
Private Collection

517 • The Postman Joseph Roulin, 1888
Oil on canvas, 65 x 54 cm
Kunstmuseum, Winterthur

518 • Portrait of Patience Escalier, Shepherd in Provence, 1888
Oil on canvas, 64 x 54 cm
Norton Simon Museum of Art, Pasadena

519 • Portrait of Patience Escalier, 1888
Oil on canvas, 69 x 56 cm
Niarchos Collection

520 • Portrait of One-eyed Man, 1888
Oil on canvas, 56 x 36.5 cm
Van Gogh Museum, Amsterdam

521 • Coal Barges, 1888
Oil on canvas, 55 x 66 cm
Museum Folkwang, Essen

522 • Coal Barges, 1888
Oil on canvas, 71 x 95 cm
Carleton Mitchell Collection, Annapolis

523 • Coal Barges, 1888
Oil on canvas, 53.5 x 64 cm
Thyssen-Bornemisza Foundation, Lugano Castagnola

524 • Lilacs, 1888
Oil on canvas, 73 x 92 cm
The Hermitage Museum, St. Petersburg

525 • Bowl with Daisies, 1888
Oil on canvas, 33 x 42 cm
National Gallery of Art, Washington

526 • Le Bouquet, 1888
Oil on canvas, 65 x 54 cm
Harriman Collection, New York

527 • Vase with Zinnias, 1888
Oil on canvas, 64 x 49.5 cm
Goulandris Collection, Lausanne

528 • Vase with Oleanders and Books, 1888
Oil on canvas, 60.3 x 73.6 cm
The Metropolitan Museum of Art, New York

513

514

515

516

517

518

519

520

521

522

523

524

525

526

527

528

529   530   531

532   533   534

535   536   537

538   539

540   541   542

543   544

529 • Vase with Five Sunflowers, 1888
Oil on canvas, 73 x 58 cm
Private Collection

530 • Vase with Twelve Sunflowers, 1888
Oil on canvas, 91 x 71 cm
Bayerische Staatsgemäldesammlungen, Neue Pinakothek, Munich

531 • The Sunflowers, 1888
Oil on canvas, 93 x 73 cm
The National Gallery, London

532 • Thistles, 1888
Oil on canvas, 59 x 49 cm
Niarchos Collection, Athens

533 • A Pair of Shoes, 1888
Oil on canvas, 44 x 53 cm
Kramarsky Trust Fund Collection, New York

534 • Self-Portrait on Tarascon Road, 1888
Oil on canvas, 48 x 44 cm

535 • Railway Carriages, 1888
Oil on canvas, 45 x 50 cm

536 • The Caravans, Gypsy Encampment Near Arles, 1888
Oil on canvas, 45 x 51 cm
Musée d'Orsay, Paris

537 • Arles: View from the Wheat Fields, 1888
Oil on canvas, 73 x 54 cm
Musée Rodin, Paris

538 • The Sower: Outskirts of Arles in the Background, 1888
Oil on canvas, 33 x 40 cm
The Armand Hammer Museum of Art, Los Angeles

539 • Farmhouses in a Wheat Field Near Arles, 1888
Oil on canvas, 24.5 x 35 cm
Van Gogh Museum, Amsterdam

540 • The Old Mill, 1888
Oil on canvas, 64.5 x 54 cm
Albright-Knox Art Gallery, Buffalo

541 • Entrance to the Public Park in Arles, 1888
Oil on canvas, 72.5 x 91 cm
The Phillips Collection, Washington

542 • Ploughed Field, 1888
Oil on canvas, 72.5 x 92.5 cm
Van Gogh Museum, Amsterdam

543 • Public Park with Weeping Willow: The Poet's Garden I, 1888
Oil on canvas, 73 x 92 cm
The Art Institute, Chicago

544 • A Lane in the Public Garden at Arles, 1888
Oil on canvas, 73 x 92 cm
Rijksmuseum Kröller-Müller, Otterlo

WORKS

545 • The Green Vineyard, 1888
Oil on canvas, 72 x 92 cm
Rijksmuseum Kröller-Müller, Otterlo

546 • The Yellow House in Arles, 1888
Oil on canvas, 79 x 94 cm
Van Gogh Museum, Amsterdam

**547 • The Night Café in the Place
Lamartine in Arles, 1888**
Oil on canvas, 70 x 89 cm
*Yale University Art Gallery,
New Haven*

548 Night Café, 1888
Oil on canvas, 81 x 65.5 cm
Rijksmuseum Kröller-Müller, Otterlo

549 • Starry Night on the Rhône, 1888
Oil on canvas, 72.5 x 92 cm
Private Collection

550 • Portrait of Eugène Boch, 1888
Oil on canvas, 60 x 45 cm
Musée d'Orsay, Paris

551 • Self-Portrait, 1888
Oil on canvas, 40 x 31 cm
Körfer Collection, Bolligen

**552 • Self-Portrait Dedicated
to Gauguin, 1888**
Oil on canvas, 60.3 x 49.4 cm
*The Fogg Art Museum, Cambridge
(Massachusetts)*

553 • Self-Portrait, 1888
Oil on canvas, 81 x 60 cm
Goetz Collection, Los Angeles

**554 • Portrait of Milliet, Second
Lieutenant of the Zouaves, 1888**
Oil on canvas, 60 x 49 cm
Rijksmuseum Kröller-Müller, Otterlo

**555 • Portrait of the Artist's
Mother, 1888**
Oil on canvas, 40.5 x 32.5 cm
Norton Simon Foundation , Fullerton

556 • Van Gogh's Room in Arles, 1888
Oil on canvas, 72 x 90 cm
Van Gogh Museum, Amsterdam

557 • Tarascon Diligence, 1888
Oil on canvas, 72 x 92 cm
Pearlman Foundation, New York

**558 • The Railway Bridge Over
Avenue Montmajour, Arles, 1888**
Oil on canvas, 71 x 92 cm
Kunsthaus, Zurich

559 • The Trinquetaille Bridge, 1888
Oil on canvas, 73.5 x 92.5 cm
Private Collection

560 • Still Life: Pears, 1888
Oil on canvas, 46 x 59.5 cm
*Gemäldegalerie, Staatliche
Kunstsammlungen, Dresden*

545

546

547

548

549

550

551

552

553

554

555

556

557

558

559

560

561

562

563

564

565

566

567

568

569

570

571

572

573

574

575

576

561 • Public Garden with Couple and Blue Fir Tree: The Poet's Garden III, 1888
Oil on canvas, 73 x 92 cm
Private Collection

562 • The Public Park at Arles, 1888
Oil on canvas, 72 x 93 cm
Private Collection

563 • The Lovers: The Poet's Garden IV, 1888
Oil on canvas, 75 x 92 cm

564 • The Sower, 1888
Oil on canvas, 72 x 91.5 cm
Jäggli-Hahnloser Collection, Winterthur

565 • The Sower, 1888
Oil on jute on canvas, 73.5 x 93 cm
Bührle Collection, Zurich

566 • The Sower, 1888
Oil on canvas, 32 x 40 cm
Van Gogh Museum, Amsterdam

567 • Trunk of an Old Yew Tree, 1888
Oil on canvas, 91 x 71 cm
National Gallery of Art, Washington

568 • Willows at Sunset, 1888
Oil on canvas, 31.5 x 34.5 cm
Rijksmuseum Kröller-Müller, Otterlo

569 • Les Alyscamps, Falling Autumn Leaves, 1888
Oil on canvas, 73 x 92 cm
Rijksmuseum Kröller-Müller, Otterlo

570 • Les Alyscamps, 1888
Oil on canvas, 72 x 91 cm
Niarchos Collection, Athens

571 • Les Alyscamps, 1888
Oil on canvas, 89 x 72 cm
Goulandris Collection, Lausanne

572 • Les Alyscamps, 1888
Oil on canvas, 92 x 73.5 cm
Private Collection

573 • The Brothel, 1888
Oil on canvas, 33 x 41 cm
The Barnes Foundation, Merion

574 • The Dance Hall in Arles, 1888
Oil on canvas, 65 x 81 cm
Musée d'Orsay, Paris

575 • Spectators at the Arena in Arles, 1888
Oil on canvas, 73 x 92 cm
The Hermitage Museum, St. Petersburg

576 • The Red Vines, 1888
Oil on canvas, 75 x 93 cm
Pushkin Museum, Moscow

WORKS

577 • Memory of the Garden in Etten, 1888
Oil on canvas, 73.5 x 92.5 cm
The Hermitage Museum,
St. Petersburg

578 • Young Man with a Cap, 1888
Oil on canvas, 47.5 x 39 cm
Private Collection

579 • Portrait of a Man, 1888
Oil on canvas, 65 x 54.5 cm
Rijksmuseum Kröller-Müller, Otterlo

580 • The Novel Reader, 1888
Oil on canvas, 73 x 92 cm
Private Collection

581 • L'Arlésienne: Madame Ginoux with Books, 1888
Oil on canvas, 91.4 x 73.7 cm
The Metropolitan Museum of Art,
New York

582 • L'Arlésienne (Madame Ginoux), 1888
Oil on canvas, 93 x 74 cm
Musée d'Orsay, Paris

583 • Portrait of Camille Roulin, 1888
Oil on canvas, 43 x 35 cm
The Museum of Art, Philadelphia

584 • Portrait of Camille Roulin, 1888
Oil on canvas, 40.5 x 32.5 cm
Van Gogh Museum, Amsterdam

585 • Portrait of Armand Roulin, 1888
Oil on canvas, 65 x 54 cm
Museum Boymans-van Beuningen,
Rotterdam

586 • Portrait of Armand Roulin, 1888
Oil on canvas, 65 x 54.5 cm
Museum Folkwang, Essen

587 • Portrait of Madame Augustine Roulin, 1888
Oil on canvas, 55 x 65 cm
Oskar Reinhart Foundation,
Winterthur

588 • Mother Roulin with Her Baby, 1888
Oil on canvas, 63.5 x 51 cm
The Metropolitan Museum of Art,
New York

589 • Mother Roulin with Her Baby, 1888
Oil on canvas, 92 x 73.5 cm
The Museum of Art, Philadelphia

590 • The Baby Marcelle Roulin, 1888
Oil on canvas, 35 x 24 cm
National Gallery of Art, Washington

591 • The Baby Marcelle Roulin, 1888
Oil on canvas, 35.5 x 24.5 cm
Van Gogh Museum, Amsterdam

592 • The Baby Marcelle Roulin, 1888
Oil on canvas, 36 x 25 cm
Socindec Foundation, Vaduz

577

578

579

580

581

582

583

584

585

586

587

588

589

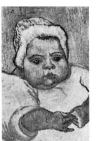
590

591

592

593

594

595

596

597

598

599

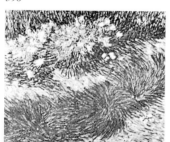

600

601

602

603

604

605

606

607

608

593 • Self-Portrait, 1888
Oil on canvas, 46 x 38 cm
Robert Lehman Foundation, New York

594 • Van Gogh's Chair, 1888
Oil on canvas, 91.8 x 73 cm
The National Gallery, London

595 • Gauguin's Chair, 1888
Oil on canvas, 90.5 x 72.5 cm
Van Gogh Museum, Amsterdam

596 • A Pair of Wooden Clogs, 1888
Oil on canvas, 32.5 x 40.5 cm
Van Gogh Museum, Amsterdam

597 • The Postman Joseph Roulin, 1888-1889
Oil on canvas, 67.5 x 56 cm
The Barnes Foundation, Merion

598 • Crab on Its Back, 1888-1889
Oil on canvas, 38 x 46.5 cm
Van Gogh Museum, Amsterdam

599 • Two Crabs, 1888-1889
Oil on canvas, 47 x 61 cm

600 • Grass and Butterflies, 1889
Oil on canvas, 51 x 61 cm
Private Collection

601 • Portrait of Doctor Félix Rey, 1889
Oil on canvas, 64 x 53 cm
Pushkin Museum, Moscow

602 • Self-Portrait with Bandaged Ear, 1889
Oil on canvas, 60 x 49 cm
Courtauld Institute Galleries, London

603 • Self-Portrait with Bandaged Ear and Pipe, 1889
Oil on canvas, 51 x 45 cm
Block Collection, Chicago

604 • Still Life: Drawing Board, Pipe, Onions, and Sealing-Wax, 1889
Oil on canvas, 50 x 64 cm
Rijksmuseum Kröller-Müller, Otterlo

605 • Still Life: Oranges, Lemons, and Blue Gloves, 1889
Oil on canvas, 47.3 x 64.3 cm
National Gallery of Art, Washington

606 • Vase with Twelve Sunflowers, 1889
Oil on canvas, 92 x 72.5 cm
The Museum of Art, Philadelphia

607 • Vase with Fourteen Sunflowers, 1889
Oil on canvas, 100.5 x 76.5 cm
Yasuda Fire & Marine Insurance Company, Tokyo

608 • Vase with Fourteen Sunflowers, 1889
Oil on canvas, 95 x 73 cm
Van Gogh Museum, Amsterdam

WORKS

609 • The Postman
Joseph Roulin, 1889
Oil on canvas, 65 x 54 cm
Rijksmuseum Kröller-Müller, Otterlo

610 • The Postman
Joseph Roulin, 1889
Oil on canvas, 64 x 54.5 cm
The Museum of Modern Art, New York

611 • The Rocking Chair
(Augustine Roulin), 1889
Oil on canvas, 93 x 74 cm
Annenberg Collection, Rancho Mirage (California)

612 • The Rocking Chair
(Augustine Roulin), 1889
Oil on canvas, 92 x 73 cm
Rijksmuseum Kröller-Müller, Otterlo

613 • The Rocking Chair
(Augustine Roulin), 1889
Oil on canvas, 93 x 73.4 cm
The Art Institute, Chicago

614 • The Rocking Chair
(Augustine Roulin), 1889
Oil on canvas, 92.7 x 72.8 cm
Museum of Fine Arts, Boston

615 • The Rocking Chair
(Augustine Roulin), 1889
Oil on canvas, 91 x 71.5 cm
Van Gogh Museum, Amsterdam

616 • Bloaters on a Piece
of Yellow Paper, 1889
Oil on canvas, 33 x 41 cm
Private Collection

617 • The Garden of the Nursing
Home at Arles, 1889
Oil on canvas, 73 x 92 cm
Oskar Reinhart Foundation, Winterthur

618 • View of Arles with
Trees in Bloom, 1889
Oil on canvas, 50.5 x 65 cm
Van Gogh Museum, Amsterdam

619 • Orchard in Bloom with
View of Arles, 1889
Oil on canvas, 72 x 92 cm
Bayerische Staatsgemäldesammlungen, Neue Pinakothek, Munich

620 • A Field of Yellow Flowers, 1889
Oil on canvas on cardboard,
34.5 x 53 cm
Kunstmuseum, Winterthur

621 • The Iris, 1889
Oil on paper on canvas, 62.5 x 48 cm
National Gallery of Canada, Ottawa

622 • La Crau with Peach
Trees in Bloom, 1889
Oil on canvas, 65.5 x 81.5 cm
Courtauld Institute Galleries, London

623 • Pollard Willows, 1889
Oil on canvas, 55 x 65 cm
Niarchos Collection, Athens

624 • Red Chestnuts in the Public
Park at Arles, 1889
Oil on canvas, 72.5 x 92 cm
Private Collection

609

610

611

612

613

614

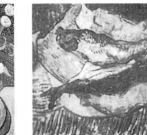
615

616

617

618

619

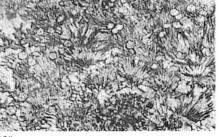
620

621

622

623

624

625

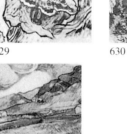

626

627

628

629

630

631

632

633

634

635

636

637

638

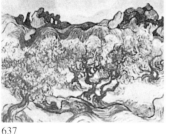

639

640

625 • The Entrance Hall of the Hôpital Saint-Paul, 1889
Gouache and black chalk on paper, 61.5 x 47.5 cm
Van Gogh Museum, Amsterdam

626 • Corridor in the Hôpital Saint-Paul, 1889
Oil on canvas, 61 x 47 cm
The Museum of Modern Art, New York

627 • The Window in Van Gogh's Bedroom, 1889
Gouache and black chalk on paper, 61.5 x 47 cm
Van Gogh Museum, Amsterdam

628 • Irises, 1889
Oil on canvas, 71 x 93 cm
The J. Paul Getty Museum, Malibu

629 • Death's-Head Moth, 1889
Oil on canvas, 33 x 24 cm
Van Gogh Museum, Amsterdam

630 • The Garden of the Hôpital Saint-Paul, 1889
Oil on canvas, 95 x 75.5 cm
Rijksmuseum Kröller-Müller, Otterlo

631 • A Corner in the Garden of the Hôpital Saint-Paul, 1889
Oil on canvas, 92 x 72 cm

632 • Portrait of a Young Peasant, 1889
Oil on canvas, 61 x 50 cm
The Solomon R. Guggenheim Foundation, Venice

633 • Mountainous Landscape Behind the Hôpital Saint-Paul, 1889
Oil on canvas, 70.5 x 88.5 cm
Ny Carlsberg Glyptotek, Copenhagen

634 • Green Wheat Field, 1889
Oil on canvas, 73 x 92 cm
Kunsthaus, Zurich

635 • Green Wheat Field with Cypress, 1889
Oil on canvas, 73.5 x 92.5 cm
Národni Galeri, Prague

636 • At the Foot of the Mountains, 1889
Oil on canvas, 37.5 x 30.5 cm
Van Gogh Museum, Amsterdam

637 • Olive Trees with the Alpilles in the Background, 1889
Oil on canvas, 72.5 x 92 cm
Whitney Collection, New York

638 • The Starry Night, 1889
Oil on canvas, 73.7 x 92.1 cm
The Museum of Modern Art, New York

639 • Cypresses, 1889
Oil on canvas, 94 x 73.3 cm
The Metropolitan Museum of Art, New York

640 • Wheat Field with Cypresses at the Haute Galline Near Eygalières, 1889
Oil on canvas, 73 x 93.5 cm
Private Collection

WORKS

641 • The Cypress and Flowering Tree, 1889
Oil on canvas, 52 x 65 cm
Private Collection

642 • Wheat Field with Cypresses, 1889
Oil on canvas, 72.5 x 91.5 cm
The National Gallery; London

643 • Wheat Fields with Reaper at Sunrise, 1889
Oil on canvas, 73 x 92 cm
Van Gogh Museum, Amsterdam

644 • Evening Landscape with Rising Moon, 1889
Oil on canvas, 72 x 92 cm
Rijksmuseum Kröller-Müller, Otterlo

645 • Entrance to a Quarry Near Saint-Rémy, 1889
Oil on canvas, 52 x 64 cm
Private Collection

646 • Mountains at Saint-Rémy with Dark Cottage, 1889
Oil on canvas, 71.8 x 90.8 cm
The Solomon R. Guggenheim Museum, New York

647 • Undergrowth with Ivy, 1889
Oil on canvas, 49 x 64 cm
Van Gogh Museum, Amsterdam

648 • Tree Trunks with Ivy, 1889
Oil on canvas, 73 x 92.5 cm
Van Gogh Museum, Amsterdam

649 • The Trunks with Ivy, 1889
Oil on canvas, 45 x 60 cm
Rijksmuseum Kröller-Müller, Otterlo

650 • Wooden Sheds, 1889
Oil on canvas, 45.5 x 60 cm
Private Collection

651 • Enclosed Field with Ploughman, 1889
Oil on canvas, 49 x 62 cm

652 • Wheat Field with Reaper and Sun, 1889
Oil on canvas, 72 x 92 cm
Rijksmuseum Kröller-Müller, Otterlo

653 • Wheat Field Behind the Hôpital Saint-Paul with a Reaper, 1889
Oil on canvas, 59.5 x 72.5 cm
Museum Folkwang, Essen

654 • Portrait of Trabuc, an Attendant at the Hôpital Saint-Paul, 1889
Oil on canvas, 61 x 46 cm
Kunstmuseum, Solothurn

641

642

643

644

645

646

647

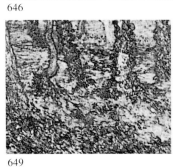
648

649

650

651

652

653

654

655   656

 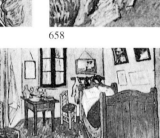 

657   658   659

660   661

662   663   664

665   666   667   668

669   670   671   672

655 • Portrait of Madame Trabuc, 1889
Oil on canvas on panel, 64 x 49 cm

656 • Self-Portrait, 1889
Oil on canvas, 57 x 43.5 cm
Whitney Collection, New York

657 • Portrait of the Artist, 1889
Oil on canvas, 65 x 54 cm
Musée d'Orsay, Paris

658 • Self-Portrait, 1889
Oil on canvas, 51 x 45 cm
Nasjonalgalleriet, Oslo

659 • Field with Ploughman and Mill, 1889
Oil on canvas, 54 x 67 cm
The Fogg Art Museum, Cambridge (Massachusetts)

660 • Van Gogh's Room in Arles, 1889
Oil on canvas, 56.5 x 74 cm
Musée d'Orsay, Paris

661 • Van Gogh's Room in Arles, 1889
Oil on canvas, 73 x 92 cm
The Art Institute, Chicago

662 • Pietà, 1889
Oil on canvas, 73 x 60.5 cm
Van Gogh Museum, Amsterdam

663 • Reaper with Sickle, 1889
Oil on canvas, 44 x 33 cm
Van Gogh Museum, Amsterdam

664 • The Reaper, 1889
Oil on canvas, 43.5 x 25 cm
Memorial Art Gallery, University of Rochester

665 • Peasant Woman with a Rake, 1889
Oil on canvas, 39 x 24 cm

666 • The Sheaf Binder, 1889
Oil on canvas, 44.5 x 32 cm
Van Gogh Museum, Amsterdam

667 • Peasant Woman Binding Sheaves, 1889
Oil on canvas, 43 x 33 cm
Van Gogh Museum, Amsterdam

668 • The Thresher, 1889
Oil on canvas, 44 x 27.5 cm
Van Gogh Museum, Amsterdam

669 • Peasant Woman Cutting Straw, 1889
Oil on canvas, 40.5 x 26.5 cm
Van Gogh Museum, Amsterdam

670 • The Sheaf Binder, 1889
Oil on canvas, 43.5 x 29.5 cm
Van Gogh Museum, Amsterdam

671 • The Spinner, 1889
Oil on canvas, 40 x 25.5 cm
Moshe Mayer Collection, Ghent

672 • The Shepherdess, 1889
Oil on canvas, 52.7 x 40.7 cm
Tel Aviv Museum, Israel

WORKS

673 • The Sower, 1889
Oil on canvas, 64 x 55 cm
Rijksmuseum Kröller-Müller, Otterlo

**674 • Peasant's House with Child
in the Cradle (The Watch), 1889**
Oil on canvas, 74.5 x 93.5 cm
Van Gogh Museum, Amsterdam

**675 • Evening: The End
of the Day, 1889**
Oil on canvas, 72 x 94 cm
Menard Art Museum, Komaki

676 • Wheat Field in Rain, 1889
Oil on canvas, 73.5 x 92.5 cm
The Museum of Art, Philadelphia

**677 • Two Poplars on a Road
Through the Hills, 1889**
Oil on canvas, 61 x 45.5 cm
The Museum of Art, Cleveland

678 • Road in the Alpilles, 1889
Oil on canvas, 55 x 45 cm
Musée d'Art Ohara, Kurashiki (Japan)

679 • La Promenade du soir, 1889
Oil on canvas, 49.5 x 45.5 cm
Museu de Arte, São Paulo

680 • Entrance to a Quarry, 1889
Oil on canvas, 60 x 73.5 cm
Van Gogh Museum, Amsterdam

681 • The Peiroulets Ravine, 1889
Oil on canvas, 31 x 40 cm
Van Gogh Museum, Amsterdam

682 • The Peiroulets Ravine, 1889
Oil on canvas, 73 x 92 cm
Museum of Fine Arts, Boston

683 • The Mulberry Tree, 1889
Oil on canvas, 54 x 65 cm
*Norton Simon Museum of Art,
Pasadena*

684 • The Walk: Falling Leaves, 1889
Oil on canvas, 73.5 x 60.5 cm
Van Gogh Museum, Amsterdam

685 • Field with Two Rabbits, 1889
Oil on canvas, 33 x 40.5 cm
Van Gogh Museum, Amsterdam

**686 • Enclosed Wheat Field
with Peasant, 1889**
Oil on canvas, 75 x 92 cm
Museum of Art, Indianapolis

**687 • Portrait of a Patient in
the Hôpital Saint-Paul, 1889**
Oil on canvas, 32.5 x 23.5 cm
Van Gogh Museum, Amsterdam

**688 • Ward in the Hospital
in Arles, 1889**
Oil on canvas, 74 x 92 cm
Fondation Oskar Reinhart, Winterthur

**689 • Trees in the Garden of
the Hôpital Saint-Paul, 1889**
Oil on canvas, 73 x 60 cm
Private Collection

673   674   675

676   677

678   679   680

681   682   683

684   685

686   687   688

689

690

691

692

693

694

695

696

697

698

699

700

701

702

703

704

**690 • Trees in the Garden of
the Hôpital Saint-Paul, 1889**
Oil on canvas, 90 x 71 cm
A. Hammer Collection, Los Angeles

**691 • The Hôpital Saint-Paul in
Saint-Rémy-de-Provence, 1889**
Oil on canvas, 63 x 48 cm
Musée d'Orsay, Paris

**692 • The Garden of the Hôpital
Saint-Paul, 1889**
Oil on canvas, 50 x 63 cm
Private Collection

**693 • The Stone Bench
in the Garden of the Hôpital
Saint-Paul, 1889**
Oil on canvas, 39 x 46 cm
Museu de Arte, São Paulo

**694 • The Garden of the Hôpital
Saint-Paul, 1889**
Gouache with black chalk and
watercolor, 37 x 61 cm
Van Gogh Museum, Amsterdam

**695 • The Garden of the Hôpital
Saint-Paul, 1889**
Oil on canvas, 71.5 x 90.5 cm
Van Gogh Museum, Amsterdam

**696 • The Garden of the Hôpital
Saint-Paul, 1889**
Oil on canvas, 73.5 x 92.6 cm
Museum Folkwang, Essen

**697 • The Garden of the Hôpital
Saint-Paul, 1889**
Oil on canvas, 64.5 x 49 cm
Private Collection

**698 • Trees in the Garden
of the Hôpital Saint-Paul, 1889**
Oil on canvas, 42 x 32 cm
Private Collection

**699 • The Garden of the Hôpital
Saint-Paul with Figure, 1889**
Oil on canvas, 61 x 50 cm
Rijksmuseum Kröller-Müller, Otterlo

700 • Study of Pine Trees, 1889
Oil on canvas, 46 x 51 cm
Rijksmuseum Kröller-Müller, Otterlo

701 • Two Diggers Among Trees, 1889
Oil on canvas, 62 x 44 cm
The Institute of Arts, Detroit

702 • Two Peasants Digging, 1889
Oil on canvas, 72 x 92 cm
Stedelijk Museum, Amsterdam

**703 • Olive Trees Against a Slope
of a Hill, 1889**
Oil on canvas, 33.5 x 40 cm
Van Gogh Museum, Amsterdam

704 • Olive Grove, 1889
Oil on canvas, 73 x 93 cm
*The Nelson Atkins Museum of Art,
Kansas City*

WORKS

**705 • Olive Grove:
Bright Blue Sky, 1889**
Oil on canvas, 45.5 x 59.5 cm
Van Gogh Museum, Amsterdam

706 • Olive Trees, 1889
Oil on canvas, 53.5 x 64.5 cm
Private Collection

**707 • Olive Trees: Bright
Blue Sky, 1889**
Oil on canvas, 49 x 63 cm
*National Gallery of Scotland,
Edinburgh*

**708 • Olive Grove:
Pale Blue Sky, 1889**
Oil on canvas, 73.5 x 91.5 cm
*Annenberg Collection, Rancho Mirage
(California)*

**709 • Olive Trees with Yellow
Sky and Sun, 1889**
Oil on canvas, 73.7 x 92.7 cm
The Institute of Arts, Minneapolis

710 • Olive Grove, 1889
Oil on canvas, 73 x 92 cm
Van Gogh Museum, Amsterdam

711 • Olive Grove, 1889
Oil on canvas, 72 x 92 cm
Rijksmuseum Kröller-Müller, Otterlo

712 • Olive Grove: Orange Sky, 1889
Oil on canvas, 74 x 93 cm
Konstmuseum, Göteborg

713 • Olive Picking, 1889
Oil on canvas, 73 x 92 cm
*The Metropolitan Museum of Art,
New York*

714 • Olive Picking, 1889
Oil on canvas, 72.4 x 89.5 cm
*Annenberg Collection, Rancho Mirage
(California)*

715 • Olive Picking, 1889
Oil on canvas, 73 x 92 cm
National Gallery of Art, Washington

**716 • Olive Grove with Picking
Figures, 1889**
Oil on canvas, 73 x 92 cm
Rijksmuseum Kröller-Müller, Otterlo

717 • Half-figure of an Angel, 1889
Oil on canvas, 54 x 64 cm

**718 • Pine Trees Against a Red Sky
with Setting Sun, 1889**
Oil on canvas, 92 x 73 cm
Rijksmuseum Kröller-Müller, Otterlo

**719 • Enclosed Field
with Rising Sun, 1889**
Oil on canvas, 71 x 90.5 cm
Private Collection

**720 • Wheat Field Behind
the Hôpital Saint-Paul, 1889**
Oil on canvas, 24 x 33.7 cm
*Virginia Museum of Fine Arts, Richmond
(Virginia)*

705

706

707

708

709

710

711

712

713

714

715

716

717

718

719

720

721

722

723

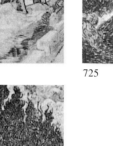

724

725

726

727

728

729

730

731

732

733

734

735

736

721 • A Meadow in the Mountains: Le Mas de Saint-Paul, 1889
Oil on canvas, 73 x 91.5 cm
Rijksmuseum Kröller-Müller, Otterlo

722 • The Peiroulets Ravine, 1889
Oil on canvas, 72 x 92 cm
Rijksmuseum Kröller-Müller, Otterlo

723 • The Road Menders, 1889
Oil on canvas, 73.5 x 92.5 cm
The Phillips Collection, Washington

724 • The Road Menders, 1889
Oil on canvas, 73.7 x 92 cm
The Museum of Art, Cleveland

725 • The White Cottage Among the Olive Trees, 1889-1890
Oil on canvas, 70 x 60 cm

726 • The Siesta, 1890
Oil on canvas, 73 x 91 cm
Musée d'Orsay, Paris

727 • Cypresses with Two Female Figures, 1889-1890
Oil on canvas, 92 x 73 cm
Rijksmuseum Kröller-Müller, Otterlo

728 • Landscape with Olive Tree and Mountains in the Background, 1890
Oil on canvas, 45 x 55 cm

729 • The Plough and the Harrow, 1890
Oil on canvas, 72 x 92 cm
Van Gogh Museum, Amsterdam

730 • First Steps, 1890
Oil on canvas, 72.4 x 91.2 cm
The Metropolitan Museum of Art, New York

731 • The Drinkers, 1890
Oil on canvas, 60 x 73 cm
The Art Institute, Chicago

732 • The Sower, 1890
Oil on canvas, 80.8 x 66 cm
Niarchos Collection, Athens

733 • The Schoolboy (Camille Roulin), 1890 (?)
Oil on canvas, 63.5 x 54 cm
Museu de Arte, São Paulo

734 • L'Arlésienne (Madame Ginoux), 1890
Oil on canvas, 60 x 50 cm
Galleria Nazionale d'Arte Moderna, Rome

735 • L'Arlésienne (Madame Ginoux), 1890
Oil on canvas, 65 x 49 cm
Rijksmuseum Kröller-Müller, Otterlo

736 • L'Arlésienne (Madame Ginoux), 1890
Oil on canvas, 65 x 54 cm
Museu de Arte, São Paulo

132

WORKS

737 • Cypresses and Two Women, 1890
Oil on canvas, 43.5 x 27 cm
Van Gogh Museum, Amsterdam

738 • Almond Trees in Blossom, 1890
Oil on canvas, 73.5 x 92 cm
Van Gogh Museum, Amsterdam

739 • Prisoners Walking, 1890
Oil on canvas, 80 x 64 cm
Pushkin Museum, Moscow

740 • The Woodcutter, 1890
Oil on canvas, 43.5 x 25 cm
Van Gogh Museum, Amsterdam

741 • Peasants Lifting Potatoes, 1890
Oil on canvas, 32 x 40.5 cm
Justin K. Thannhauser Foundation, New York

742 • L'Arlésienne (Madame Ginoux), 1890
Oil on canvas, 66 x 54 cm
Private Collection

743 • Two Peasant Women Digging in Field with Snow, 1890
Oil on canvas, 50 x 64 cm
Bührle Collection, Zurich

744 • Thatched Cottages in the Sunshine: Reminiscence of the North, 1890
Oil on canvas, 50 x 39 cm
The Barnes Foundation, Merion

745 • Cottages: Reminiscence of the North, 1890
Oil on canvas, 45.5 x 43 cm
Private Collection

746 • Cottages and Cypresses: Reminiscence of the North, 1890
Oil on canvas on panel, 29 x 36.5 cm
Van Gogh Museum, Amsterdam

747 • Valley with Ploughman Seen from Above, 1890
Oil on canvas, 33 x 41 cm

748 • View of the Alpilles, 1890
Oil on canvas, 59 x 72 cm
Rijksmuseum Kröller-Müller, Otterlo

749 • Landscape in the Neighborhood of Saint-Rémy, 1890
Oil on canvas, 33 x 41 cm

750 • Pine Trees and Dandelions in the Garden of the Hôpital Saint-Paul, 1890
Oil on canvas, 72 x 90 cm
Rijksmuseum Kröller-Müller, Otterlo

751 • Meadow in the Garden of the Hôpital Saint-Paul, 1890
Oil on canvas, 64.5 x 81 cm
The National Gallery, London

752 • Two White Butterflies, 1890
Oil on canvas, 54 x 46 cm
Van Gogh Museum, Amsterdam

737

738

739

740

741

742

743

744

745

746

747

748

749

750

751

752

753

754

755

756

757

758

759

760

761

762

763

764

765

766

767

768

753 • The Fenced-off Field, 1890
Oil on canvas, 72 x 92 cm
Rijksmuseum Kröller-Müller, Otterlo

754 • Field with Poppies, 1890
Oil on canvas, 71 x 91 cm
Kunsthalle, Bremen

755 • Landscape with Trees and Figures, 1890
Oil on canvas, 50 x 65.4 cm
The Museum of Art, Baltimore

756 • A Road at Saint-Rémy with Female Figure, 1890
Oil on canvas, 32.5 x 40.5 cm
Private Collection

757 • Road with Cypress and Star, 1890
Oil on canvas, 92 x 73 cm
Rijksmuseum Kröller-Müller, Otterlo

758 • Mount Gaussier, 1890
Oil on canvas, 53 x 70 cm
Private Collection

759 • The Good Samaritan, 1890
Oil on canvas, 73 x 60 cm
Rijksmuseum Kröller-Müller, Otterlo

760 • The Raising of Lazarus, 1890
Oil on canvas, 50 x 65 cm
Van Gogh Museum, Amsterdam

761 • Still Life: Vase with Roses, 1890
Oil on canvas, 71 x 90 cm
Averell Collection, New York

762 • White Roses, 1890
Oil on canvas, 93 x 72 cm
Annenberg Collection, Rancho Meriage (California)

763 • Still Life: Vase with Irises, 1890
Oil on canvas, 73.7 x 93 cm
The Metropolitan Museum of Art, New York

764 • Vase with Irises Against a Yellow Background, 1890
Oil on canvas, 92 x 73.5 cm
Van Gogh Museum, Amsterdam

765 • On the Threshold of Eternity, 1890
Oil on canvas, 81 x 65 cm
Rijksmuseum Kröller-Müller, Otterlo

766 • The Little Stream, 1890
Oil on canvas, 25.5 x 34 cm
Private Collection

767 • Poppies and Butterflies, 1890
Oil on canvas, 34.5 x 25.5 cm
Van Gogh Museum, Amsterdam

768 • Roses and Beetle, 1890
Oil on canvas, 33.5 x 24.5 cm
Van Gogh Museum, Amsterdam

769 • Wild Roses, 1890
Oil on canvas, 24.5 x 33 cm
Van Gogh Museum, Amsterdam

770 • Pink Roses, 1890
Oil on canvas, 32 x 40.5 cm
Ny Carlsberg Glyptotek, Copenhagen

771 • Thatched Cottages, 1890
Oil on canvas, 60 x 73 cm
*The Hermitage Museum,
St. Petersburg*

772 • Chestnut Trees in Bloom, 1890
Oil on canvas, 70 x 58 cm
Private Collection

773 • Chestnut Trees in Bloom, 1890
Oil on canvas, 63 x 50.5 cm
Rijksmuseum Kröller-Müller, Otterlo

**774 • Blooming Chestnut
Branches, 1890**
Oil on canvas, 72 x 91 cm
Bührle Collection, Zurich

775 • View the l'Oise, 1890
Gouache with pencil and watercolor,
47.5 x 63 cm
The Tate Gallery, London

776 • The House of Père Pilon, 1890
Oil on canvas, 49 x 70 cm
Niarchos Collection

**777 • Doctor Gachet's Garden
at Auvers-sur-Oise, 1890**
Oil on canvas, 73 x 51.5 cm
Musée d'Orsay, Paris

**778 • Marguerite Gachet
in the Garden, 1890**
Oil on canvas, 46 x 55.5 cm
Musée d'Orsay, Paris

779 • Doctor Paul Gachet, 1890
Oil on canvas, 68 x 57 cm
Musée d'Orsay, Paris

780 • Doctor Paul Gachet, 1890
Oil on canvas, 66 x 57 cm
Ryoei Saito Collection, Tokyio

781 • The Church at Auvers, 1890
Oil on canvas, 94 x 74.5 cm
Musée d'Orsay, Paris

**782 • View of Auvers
with Church, 1890**
Oil on canvas, 34 x 42 cm
*Museum of Art, Rhode Island School
of Design, Providence*

**783 • Wheat Fields with Auvers
in the Background, 1890**
Oil on canvas, 43 x 50 cm
Private Collection

784 • Pietà, 1890 (1889?)
Oil on canvas, 42 x 34 cm
*Bernhard C. Solomon Collection,
Los Angeles*

769

770

771

772

773

774

775

776

777

778

779

780

781

782

783

784

785

786

787

788

789

790

791

792

793

794

795

796

797

798

799

800

**785 • Thatched Cottages
in Jorgus, 1890**
Oil on canvas, 33 x 40.5 cm
*Reader's Digest Collection,
Pleasantville (New York)*

786 • Houses in Auvers, 1890
Oil on canvas, 60.6 x 73 cm
Museum of Art, Toledo (Ohio)

**787 • Houses with Thatched Roofs,
Cordeville, 1890**
Oil on canvas, 73 x 92 cm
Musée d'Orsay, Paris

**788 • Landscape with Carriage and
Train in the Background, 1890**
Oil on canvas, 72 x 90 cm
Pushkin Museum, Moscow

**789 • Vineyards with a View
of Auvers, 1890**
Oil on canvas, 64 x 80 cm
The Art Museum, Saint Louis

790 • Blooming Acacia Branches, 1890
Oil on canvas, 32.5 x 24 cm
Nationalmuseum, Stockholm

791 • Ears of Wheat, 1890
Oil on canvas, 64.5 x 48.5 cm
Van Gogh Museum, Amsterdam

**792 • Vase with Flower
and Thistles, 1890**
Oil on canvas, 41 x 34 cm
Private Collection

**793 • Wildflowers and Thistles
in a Vase, 1890**
Oil on paper on canvas,
67 x 47 cm
Private Collection

794 • Red Poppies and Daisies, 1890
Oil on canvas, 65 x 50 cm
Albright-Knox Art Gallery, Buffalo

795 • Vase with Rose-mallows, 1890
Oil on canvas, 42 x 29 cm
Van Gogh Museum, Amsterdam

796 • Roses and Anemones, 1890
Oil on canvas, 51 x 51 cm
Musée d'Orsay, Paris

797 • Glass with Carnations, 1890
Oil on canvas, 41 x 32 cm
Private Collection

798 • Glass with Wildflowers, 1890
Oil on canvas, 41 x 34 cm
*Reader's Digest Collection,
Pleasantville (New York)*

**799 • Wheat Field at Auvers with
White House, 1890**
Oil on canvas, 48.5 x 63 cm
The Phillips Collection, Washington

800 • Daubigny's Garden, 1890
Oil on canvas, 50.7 x 50.7 cm
Van Gogh Museum, Amsterdam

WORKS

801 • Field with Poppies, 1890
Oil on canvas, 73 x 91.5 cm
Haags Gemeentemuseum, The Hague

802 • Garden with Sunflowers, 1890
Oil on panel, 31.5 x 41 cm
Private Collection

803 • Child with Orange, 1890
Oil on canvas, 50 x 51 cm
Jäggli-Hahnloser Collection,
Winterthur

804 • Two Sulky Children, 1890
Oil on canvas, 51.2 x 51 cm
Musée d'Orsay, Paris

805 • Two Smiling Children, 1890
Oil on canvas, 51.5 x 46.5 cm
Goulandris Collection, Lausanne

806 • Young Girl Standing Against
a Background of Wheat, 1890
Oil on canvas, 66 x 45 cm
National Gallery of Art, Washington

807 • Young Peasant Woman with
Straw Hat Sitting in the Wheat, 1890
Oil on canvas, 92 x 73 cm
Hahnloser Collection, Bern

808 • Portrait of Adeline Ravoux, 1890
Oil on canvas, 67 x 55 cm
Private Collection

809 • Portrait of Adeline Ravoux, 1890
Oil on canvas, 52 x 52 cm
The Museum of Art, Cleveland

810 • Portrait of Adeline Ravoux, 1890
Oil on canvas, 73.7 x 54.7 cm
Private Collection

811 • Marguerite Gachet
at the Piano, 1890
Oil on canvas, 102.6 x 50 cm
Kunstmuseum, Basel

812 • Bank of the Oise at Auvers, 1890
Oil on canvas, 73.3 x 93.7 cm
The Institute of Arts, Detroit

813 • The White House at Night, 1890
Oil on canvas, 59.5 x 73 cm

801

802

803

804

805

806

807

808

809

810

811

812

813

814

815

816

817

818

819

820

821

822

823

824

814 • The Grove, 1890
Oil on canvas, 73 x 92 cm
Hazen Collection, New York

815 • Landscape with the Château of Auvers at Sunset, 1890
Oil on canvas, 50 x 101 cm
Van Gogh Museum, Amsterdam

816 • Undergrowth with Two Figures, 1890
Oil on canvas, 50 x 100 cm
The Art Museum, Cincinnati

817 • Wheat Fields Near Auvers, 1890
Oil on canvas, 50 x 101 cm
Österreichische Galerie im Belvedere, Vienna

818 • View of the Church of Saint-Paul-de-Mausole, 1890 (1889?)
Oil on canvas, 44.5 x 60 cm
Formerly Taylor Collection, Gstaad

819 • The House of Père Eloi, 1890
Oil on canvas, 51 x 58 cm
Private Collection

820 • View of Auvers, 1890
Oil on canvas, 50 x 52 cm
Van Gogh Museum, Amsterdam

821 • Houses in Auvers, 1890
Oil on canvas, 73 x 60.5 cm
Museum of Fine Arts, Boston

822 • Village Street in Auvers, 1890
Oil on canvas, 73 x 92 cm
Ateneumin Taidemuseo, Helsinki

823 • Cows, 1890
Oil on canvas, 55 x 65 cm
Musée des Beaux-Arts, Lille

824 • View of Vessenots Near Auvers, 1890
Oil on canvas, 55 x 65 cm
Hahnloser-Gassmann Collection, Zurich

WORKS

825 • Garden in Auvers, 1890
Oil on canvas, 64 x 80 cm
Private Collection

826 • The Fields, 1890
Oil on canvas, 50 x 65 cm
Private Collection

827 • Green Wheat Fields, 1890
Oil on canvas, 73 x 93 cm
National Gallery of Art, Washington

**828 • Wheat Field
with Cornflowers, 1890**
Oil on canvas, 60 x 81 cm
Private Collection

829 • Field with Wheatstacks, 1890
Oil on canvas, 50 x 100 cm
Hahnloser Collection, Bern

830 • Sheaves of Wheat, 1890
Oil on canvas, 50.5 x 101 cm
Museum of Art, Dallas

**831 • Wheat Field Under
Clouded Sky, 1890**
Oil on canvas, 50 x 100 cm
Van Gogh Museum, Amsterdam

832 • Wheat Field with Crows, 1890
Oil on canvas, 50.5 x 100.5 cm
Van Gogh Museum, Amsterdam

**833 • Landscape at Auvers
in the Rain, 1890**
Oil on canvas, 50 x 100.5 cm
National Museum of Wales, Cardiff

834 • Daubigny's Garden, 1890
Oil on canvas, 53 x 103 cm
The Art Museum, Hiroshima

835 • Daubigny's Garden, 1890
Oil on canvas, 54 x 101.5 cm
Kunstmuseum, Basel

**836 • Auvers Town Hall
on 14 July 1890, 1890**
Oil on canvas, 72 x 93 cm
Private Collection

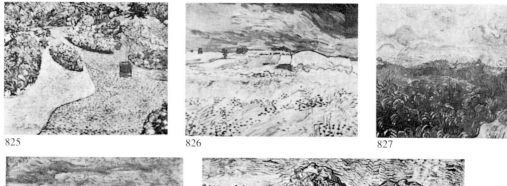

825 826 827

828 829

830

831 832

833 834

835 836

837

838

839

840

837 • Landscape with Three Trees and a House, 1890
Oil on canvas, 64 x 78 cm
Rijksmuseum Kröller-Müller, Otterlo

838 • Thatched Cottages by a Hill, 1890
Oil on canvas, 50 x 100 cm
The Tate Gallery, London

839 • Farmhouse with Two Figures, 1890
Oil on canvas, 38 x 45 cm
Van Gogh Museum, Amsterdam

840 • Two Women Crossing the Fields, 1890
Oil on paper on canvas, 30.3 x 59.7 cm
The Marion Koogler McNay Art Institute, San Antonio

841 • Village Street and Steps in Auvers with Two Figures, 1890
Oil on canvas, 20.5 x 26 cm
The Museum of Art, Hiroshima

842 • Village Street and Steps in Auvers with Figures, 1890
Oil on canvas, 49.8 x 70.1 cm
The Art Museum, Saint Louis

843 • Thatched Sandstone Cottages in Chaponval, 1890
Oil on canvas, 65 x 81 cm
Kunsthaus, Zurich

844 • Wheat Fields at Auvers Under Clouded Sky, 1890
Oil on canvas, 73 x 92 cm
Carnegie Institute, Museum of Art, Pittsburgh

845 • Plain Near Auvers, 1890
Oil on canvas, 73.5 x 92 cm
Bayerische Staatsgëmaldesammlungen, Neue Pinakothek, Munich

846 • Plain Near Auvers, 1890
Oil on canvas, 50 x 40 cm

847 • The Roots and Trunks, 1890
Oil on canvas, 50 x 100 cm
Van Gogh Museum, Amsterdam

841

842

843

844

845

846

847

Bibliography

The Complete Letters of Vincent Van Gogh, 3 vols., London, 1958

A. ARTHAUD, *Van Gogh le suicidé de la société*, Paris, 1947

P. BONAFOUX, *Van Gogh le soleil en face*, (Découverte Gallimard), Paris, 1987

P. CABANNE, *Van Gogh, l'homme et son œuvre*, Paris, 1961

F. ELGAR, *Van Gogh*, Paris, 1958

J.-B. DE LA FAILLE, *The Works of Vincent Van Gogh: His Paintings and Drawings*, Amsterdam-New York, 1970

A.M. ET R. HAMMACHER, *Van Gogh, a Documentary Biography*, London, 1982

J. HULSKER, *The Complete Van Gogh. Paintings, Drawings, Sketches*, Oxford-New York, 1980

K. JASPERS, *Strindberg und van Gogh. Versuch einer pathographischen Analyse unter vergleichender Heranziehung von Swedenborg und Hölderin*, Munich, 1949

P. LECALDANO, *Tout l'œuvre peint de Van Gogh 1881-1888,* Paris, 1971; *1888-1890,* Paris, 1971

J. REWALD, *Post-Impressionism - From Van Gogh to Gauguin*, New York, 1978

M. ROSKILL, *Van Gogh, Gauguin, and the Impressionist Circle*, Greenwich, 1970

M. SHAPIRO, *Vincent Van Gogh*, New York, 1950

E. VAN UITERS, M. HOYLE, *The Rijksmuseum Vincent Van Gogh*, Amsterdam, 1987

Van Gogh à Paris, catalogue of the Exhibition, Musée d'Orsay, Paris, 1988

Van Gogh in St. Rémy and Auvers, catalogue of the Exhibition, The Metropolitan Museum of Art, New York, 1984

Vincent Van Gogh and the Birth of Cloisonisme, B. Welsh-Ovcharov, ed., catalogue of the Exhibition, Toronto-Amsterdam, 1981

R. WALLACE, *The World of Van Gogh*, New York, 1969

I.F. WALTHER, R. METZGER, *Vincent Van Gogh. The Complete Paintings*, 2 vols., Cologne, 1990

Picture Credits

AISA, ARCHIVO ICONOGRÁFICO, S.A., Barcelona
4, 8, 9, 14, 15, 16, 30, 31, 32, 33, 42, 43, 44, 45, 50, 51, 52, 53, 56, 57, 58, 59, 60, 61, 62, 63, 64, 65, 66, 67, 68, 69, 70, 71, 72, 73, 74, 75, 76, 77, 78, 79, 80,81

GIRAUDON, Paris
22

MUSÉE RODIN, Paris
34, 35

MUSEUM OF FINE ARTS, Boston
40,41

ROGER-VIOLLET, Paris
5, 6, 10, 11, 12, 13, 17, 18, 19, 20, 21, 23,

THE DETROIT INSTITUTE OF ARTS, Detroit
38, 39

THE FOGG ART MUSEUM, HARVARD UNIVERSITY ART MUSEUMS, Cambridge (Massachusetts)
46, 47

THE METROPOLITAN MUSEUM OF ART, New York
36, 37

THE NATIONAL GALLERY, London
54, 55

VAN GOGH MUSEUM, VINCENT VAN GOGH FOUNDATION, Amsterdam
7, 26, 27, 28, 29, 48, 49, 82, 83

VON DER HEYDT-MUSEUM, Wuppertal
24, 25

The publisher wishes to express gratitude to the photographer,
Alfredo Dagli Orti, for his valuable collaboration.